THE EPISODE GUIDE

The Classic Episodes

THE EPISODE GUIDE

The Classic Episodes

based on the Universal Television series "Sliders"
created by Tracy Tormé & Robert K. Weiss.

Brad Linaweaver

New York

Sliders: The Episode Guide is based on the Universal Television series "Sliders" created by Tracy Tormé & Robert K. Weiss.

Publisher's Cataloging-in-Publication Data
Linaweaver, Brad, 1952-
    Sliders : the episode guide / Brad Linaweaver.—1st ed.
      p. cm.
    ISBN: 1-57500-053-9
    1. Sliders (Television program) 2. Science fiction television programs. I. Title.
    PN1992.77.S55L56 1998   791.45'72
                                        QBI98-66765

TV Books, L.L.C.
Publishers serving the television industry.
1619 Broadway, Ninth Floor
New York, NY 10019
www.tvbooks.com

Dedicated to KEN STEADMAN

ACKNOWLEDGMENTS

Thanks to Vanessa Koman, Jerry O'Connell's No. 1 fan, for invaluable help with the interviews.

Thanks also to the creators and stars who cooperated above and beyond the call of duty, and to: Cindy Chang, Senior Director of Universal Studios Publishing Rights; Robyn Feldman, assistant to the line producer; Meta Puttkamer, the second AD (assistant director); Lydia Marano of Dangerous Visions who did the *Sliders* cards; Thomas Cron for his vast knowledge of alternate histories; Jeremy Smith for doing the lion's share of the show bible; Nigel Mitchell for listing my novel in the *Technical Manual*; Victor and Veronica, Vanessa's parents; Gail Higgins for being such a great computer troubleshooter; James 'Greg' Condon and Ed Kramer for treating the series, and me, so well at their science-fiction conventions; Bill Ritch for making me watch my first episodes of both *Doctor Who* and *Sliders*; Peter Spellos for being the first to tell me what it was like to work on *Sliders*; and, finally, to the good folk at the Ashley Grayson Literary Agency—Herr Ashley himself, his lovely wife Carolyn, and diligent, daring Dan Hooker.

"The only thing funnier than history is physics."

— Chauntecleer Michael

CONTENTS

PART ONE:
WHAT IS SLIDING?

After taking a deep breath, Quinn hit the record button and stood in front of the camera. He unlocked a drawer and removed a small device that looked like a remote control. It could have been part of the video equipment, but it wasn't. He turned it on.

In the center of the room there was a whooshing sound.

Something happened to the air. It tasted funny. Next came a crackling sound followed by static electricity that made his hair stand on end.

Something unearthly formed before his face, right out of thin air, about five feet off the ground. The object was doughnut-shaped. At first it had the texture of a purple smoke ring—shimmering, diaphanous, reflective. Then it took on a harder appearance with a diameter of nearly six feet. The dominant color was blue, spreading out as if ink had been dropped in a pool of water.

He didn't feel the tug from the circle until the whirlpool effect began; and then there was a rushing wind, sucking at him, pulling at his hair and his clothes, beckoning him to enter. . . .

A tunnel. At first glance, the three-dimensional effect was the most startling aspect of Quinn's "monster." He walked around the shimmering blue thing suspended in the center of his basement and discovered that the damned thing was actually two-dimensional.

Faced head-on, it was a tunnel leading to God-knows-where. But if you walked to the side it simply disappeared . . . for a fraction of an instant. Because if you kept walking it reappeared again from the other side. From that angle, it became a shimmering circle of water distortion effects through which you could see the wall of the basement as if peering through the thick glass of an aquarium.

He never tired of looking at the rippling shapes in the fun house. From this side, everything he saw was known. On the other side was the unknown.

∞   ∞   ∞

This was how I described the vortex in the first chapter of my novel (*Sliders: The Novel*). In the script, Quinn says, "My attempt to create the world's first anti-gravity device has taken a decidedly bizarre turn."

This is a spectacular example of serendipity. One of the hallmarks of genius is to know what to make of an opportunity. Quinn already has a theory of parallel time tracks—of alternate worlds. He's ready to make the journey.

Sliders is the world's first television series about allohistory, a fancy name for alternate histories whose fun is in wondering how history might have taken a different path.

The portrayal of sliding was a tour-de-force for the special effects department. Here's what I think sliding would feel like (again from the novel):

∞   ∞   ∞

He took one small step into the void. He heard the sounds before he could see anything. At first it was a rushing and roaring torrent of air, as if plummeting down a wind tunnel at terrific speed. But he didn't have the stomach-turning-over feeling, or the heart-in-his-throat sensation. It was as if his body were being spread thinner and thinner while he didn't actually move at all.

As he began to see visual impressions, a blur of chaotic colors, the sound took on the quality of discordant music. Was he being tempted by some kind of Pied Piper to enter the tunnel?

And now he could see. The "music" sounded like waves crashing on a beach as he finally made out a shape up ahead: a bending focal point of light. A prism. The sight made him feel as if he might be tumbling straight toward it—while at the same time he felt that he wasn't moving at all. His mind stretched as if made from Silly Putty. Then he was in the heart of the light, as the world exploded around him in a plethora of brilliant colors.

A word was floating in his brain, but he didn't know if he was thinking of the word or becoming the word: awesome. Now he had the sensation of swimming through a pulsing array of greens, yellows, blues, reds—but he did not so much see each color as experience what it was like to be it.

The part of him that was Quinn Mallory remembered what it was like to ride on a roller coaster or go down a water slide. He wanted to shout in order to release the tension; but the disembodied mind he was, at this moment, had forgotten how to shout.

Shapes of light. Flavors of darkness. He was at the center of the universe; and the entire universe was pouring through him at some narrow little point where his eyes used to be. If he survived this, he wondered if sex would ever be the same for him again.

Everything was in flux. And then he was back in a blue tunnel, back in his body...with a falling sensation. A very pronounced falling sensation! He was going faster and faster and faster. He was certain that he was going to die.

Nothing could have been more anti-climatic than coming to rest, with a mild bump, in the center of his own basement. As the shock subsided and he took in his surroundings, the exhilaration he'd felt a moment before vanished as completely as the blue vortex, which started fading out of existence, the trip over. One ride to a customer.

∞   ∞   ∞

This is the scene in the pilot episode in which Quinn believes that he has failed big time. Of course, he succeeded beyond his wildest dreams by sliding to an alternate Earth. Establishing a principle the series would follow religiously for two seasons, he is still in San Francisco—a different San Francisco.

Unlike so many science-fiction shows in which the heroes wind up in an environment where no one would speak colloquial English, except that the plot requires it, *Sliders* avoids this problem by its very premise. If so many other things are parallel, it is reasonable to assume that most of the time the language will be a similar kind of English.

Granting the existence of parallel universes, sliding would be a means of getting from one universe to another. The pilot episode mentions the Einstein-Rosen-Podolsky bridge. Here's a longer lecture:

Gravity warps space; and the greater the gravity field, the more warpage. In our universe (this space-time continuum), the only object with sufficient gravity to cause an opening to Somewhere Else is a black hole, a collapsed star with such an intense gravity field that not even light can escape its embrace.

The idea of the bridge is that anyone who could enter this area would find a wormhole and, voila, a one-way ticket to another universe. The problem is that anyone foolhardy enough to try this in a spaceship, say, would be torn to pieces and crushed. Annihilation barely describes the experience one would have in a black hole.

Bad idea, huh? Better to vacation somewhere else. Only a crazy science-fiction writer would even dream of how to get around such an insurmountable problem. I've always thought the "event horizon" refers to the special-effects event that would occur to unlucky spaceships.

The solution was suggested by mathematician Roy Kerr. Working on the hypothesis that black holes spin on an axis, Kerr suggested the phenomenon would be analogous to the eye of a hurricane. There would be a second event horizon where humans could safely enter.

Rather than pretend I understand equations, I'll stick with metaphors, the writer's stock-in-trade. We've done whirlpools and hurricanes. Here's another. If you're sailing and a strong wind comes up, you're not going to try to sail directly into the wind. You'll tack instead (referring to the position of a vessel relative to the trim of its sails). As Francis Bacon told us, before we can command Nature we must obey her.

In *Sliders*, Quinn was working on an anti-gravity device. The energies he released created a tunnel of some kind of super-matter, a substance so powerful that it can resist the forces previously discussed in the example of the black hole and the spaceship.

Every time that shimmering blue funnel appears, two universes are temporarily linked and living things can travel between Point A and Point B. Whatever power is being used to keep this gateway open can only do so for a brief time and then the tunnel collapses into nothing. After a lifetime of reading science fiction, I couldn't help but imagine scenarios in which events might have developed in a far less satisfactory manner. During the Manhattan Project, some of the scientists considered the admittedly long-shot possibility that the detonation of the first nuclear device might set up a chain reaction in the atmosphere that would effectively destroy the world. Considering the forces with which Quinn is playing, he might have destroyed the solar system! The most powerful hydrogen bomb is a toy next to the forces required to slide.

The sliding machine is in Quinn's basement. The device the traveler takes with him is not actually given an official name on the show except for the timing attachment, which is quite naturally called a timer. The device serves two functions, telling them when they will next slide and also opening the gateway. The sliding machine is controlled by the timer the same way a remote control programs a VCR. There is a display so the Slider knows how much time he has on the latest parallel Earth before he has to leave.

On the first test run, Quinn gave himself a pre-programmed amount of time, at the end of which the vortex opened up automatically and sucked him home. This would ideally be the way he'd take every trip, but in the grand old tradition of adventure stories, something went wrong . . . terribly wrong.

In the pilot episode, the calculations are thrown off and the timing device's preset controls are wiped out. Quinn rebuilds the timer/gizmo with help from Arturo, but has no way of replacing the erased programming. During his test slide, the timer was programmed with the location of "Home." The sliding machine can keep opening up gateways for them to visit new Earths, but the travelers have no way of telling it which dimension is their original Earth.

The amount of time they spend on each new Earth is as random as the places they visit. The timer is now a countdown device informing them how much time they have in each new world before they must slide again. The time frames vary wildly from minutes to months, but not years. However, if they miss the preordained exit, they will be stuck wherever they've wound up for 29.7 years. After that, the gateway returns.

The assumption is that the universes themselves travel, and just as planets have times of being closer to each other than other times, so it is with the parallel worlds. As to why they keep wandering into worlds with a San Francisco and various versions of themselves, there is no ultimate explanation but plenty of theorizing for Sliders (the fans) to engage in on the Internet. With the third season, all of California becomes their playground.

Maybe they are linked somehow to worlds in which there exists something of themselves. In some episodes they will meet one or two analogs of themselves, some none. But I wouldn't be surprised to learn that every single Earth they visit has some version of all four, even if they don't meet them, even if their analogs all died at birth.

They've become so spoiled by the Golden Gate Bridge that it is always a grim moment when they land in a version of San Francisco without it or where it's decorated in goblins or colored blue!

Before wrapping up this section on hard science (I prefer easy science), I'll quote again from my book:

∞   ∞   ∞

According to quantum physics, there is no such thing as absolute time. There is only relative time—relative to the location and speed of the observer. Simultaneity is a theoretical concept positing that if time is a single line, two events might be said to occur at the same point on that line.

Time, however, is not a single, neat line. Professor Arturo refers to it as a corkscrew.

Which brings us to the subject of Rembrandt Brown.

∞   ∞   ∞

That segue was there because Rembrandt was about to be thoroughly screwed by becoming one of the Sliders instead of making an important singing gig. The issues raised are food for thought for those who take the show seriously enough to wonder why the Sliders are in some kind of strange, cross-dimensional temporal trap.

This is the scene in which the fabulous foursome first funnel together. Quinn, Wade, and Arturo know what's happening. Poor Rembrandt Brown, the Crying Man, has reason to cry because he has no idea what he's driven into. When the vortex appears in front of him, he thinks he's seeing a giant blue platter. Naturally a professional singer would think of a record. He's about to top the cosmic charts.

Returning to Quinn, we learn:

∞   ∞   ∞

Traveling alone through the wormhole had been a trip-and-a-half. Now Quinn concluded that traveling with others gave the experience a whole new dimension (in a manner of speaking). It was like he received all of Wade and Arturo's impressions, but this in no way diminished him. Everyone did not merge into one identity, yet each person's identity became part of the others' living background and experience. He tasted their minds.

There was another weird aspect to the experience. From his perspective, he didn't have a body—but he could see the physical shapes of the others as if they were bumping around in a zero-g chamber. Or maybe they were swimming.

The most dramatic difference from the last slide was Quinn's impression of seeing a howling banshee driving a red Cadillac, headed straight for the increasingly brilliant prism of light that must be the terminus of the journey. This was better, he concluded, than seeing Mary Poppins taking a joyride through the tunnel.

Then multicolored lights washed away all disturbing details. There was the sound of rushing wind that was not wind and the terrible sensation that told him again, in no uncertain terms, that he had a body of flesh and blood. Especially blood.

∞   ∞   ∞

Hey, it hurts when you hit the ground hard.

PART TWO:
WHO ARE
THE SLIDERS?

QUINN MALLORY is quite possibly the smartest man in the world. Young, brave, super-intelligent, he holds the key to sliding—a technology he developed in a home-made laboratory in his basement. This allows him to visit parallel Earths where he occasionally encounters other versions of himself, who may be the smartest guys in their worlds.

JERRY O'CONNELL plays the role. His acting career began at the age of eleven in the film *Stand by Me*. He grew up on camera, working in television commercials and numerous series. Since starring in *Sliders*, he has appeared in the feature films *Joe's Apartment, Jerry Maguire*, and *Scream 2*. A native New Yorker, O'Connell is a graduate of NYU, where he majored in film and television. He was a member of the university's saber-fencing team. He was born on February 17, 1974.

∞   ∞   ∞

WADE KATHLEEN WELLES is Quinn's smart, delightful friend who wants to be more than just a friend (this seems to vary)—but for now must be content going on a series of incredible adventures. She is also a whiz at computers but is far too cute to be a nerd.

SABRINA LLOYD plays the role. From the age of twelve, she knew that she wanted to be an actress. She moved from doing community theater in Eustis, Florida, to her first feature film appearance in *Chain of Desire*. This led to a starring role in *Fatherhood* and to television work. She divides her time between New York and L.A., and her birth date is November 11.

(NOTE: Since the completion of this book, Sabrina Lloyd has left *Sliders*. Her new show is *Sports Night* on ABC.)

∞ ∞ ∞

REMBRANDT LEE "CRYING MAN" BROWN is a member of the classic R&B group the Spinning Topps. A top-drawer en-tertainer, he is known for crying real tears at his performances. On the way to a come-back gig, he makes a slight detour and winds up playing to audiences in parallel worlds, sometimes enjoying greater success than he ever had back home.

CLEAVANT DERRICKS plays the role. He decided to become an actor when it occurred to him that while all his friends were playing sports, he wanted to perform in front of the camera. Starting his career in theater, he performed with local tours, then off-Broadway productions, later winning a Tony award for his performance in *Dreamgirls*. His Broadway credits include *Jesus Christ Superstar*. Derricks currently resides in Agoura Hills, CA, and his birth date is May 15.

∞ ∞ ∞

PROFESSOR MAXIMILLIAN P. ARTURO is a brilliant, skeptical, irascible older man who is given a graduate course in life by his young genius student. He provides an anchor of sanity in some of their wilder situations.

JOHN RHYS-DAVIES plays the role. A bona-fide movie star, the acclaimed Welsh actor is best known for his work in *Raiders of the Lost Ark; Indiana Jones and the Last Cru-*  *sade; Victor, Victoria; King Solomon's Mines;* and the James Bond movie, *The Living Daylights*. Growing up in England, Africa, and Wales, he was exposed to classic literature leading him to pursue a theatrical career. After refining his craft at London's renowned Royal Academy of Dramatic Arts, he moved on to work in television, radio, and, of course, legitimate theater. He divides his time between Los Angeles and the Isle of Man. His birth date is May 5, 1944. He may be seen as Leonardo da Vinci on *Star Trek: Voyager*.

(Note: Since the completion of this book, John Rhys-Davies has left the show.)

∞ ∞ ∞

CAPTAIN MAGGIE BECKETT is a former fighter pilot, now an intelligence officer in the military establishment. She is a strong-willed individual who, although occasionally detached and pragmatic, possesses passion and selflessness when defending the lives of her fellow Sliders. Captain Maggie joined in with the Sliders to seek justice after Rickman aided in destroying her home planet and killing her husband.

KARI WUHRER plays the role. Her career took off in 1989 when she caught the attention of MTV and the producers of their innovative game show *Remote Control*. After leaving MTV, she moved to Los Angeles where she landed a principal role as Robin Farr on Fox Network's *Class of '96*. Wuhrer emerged as a big success on the show and moved on to a recurring role on *Beverly Hills 90210*. Kari's latest projects include *Higher Learning, Anaconda,* and *Sex and the Single Man*.

∞   ∞   ∞

As 1996 drew to a close, I had the privilege of going onto the set of *Sliders* to watch some of the filming of the episode, "Murder Most Foul." The second AD (Assistant Director), Meta Puttkammer, was a doll, helping facilitate interviews with the stars.

Robyn Feldman, assistant to the Line Producer, made the arrangements and allowed me to bring along a guest, Vanessa Koman, daughter of one of my best friends. A few months away from her thirteenth birthday, and an actress herself since the age of ten, she was currently starring in a Fred Olen Ray production, *Little Miss Magic*. Between the two of us, I was more likely to blow a take by stumbling over something or making a noise. She's a lot more mature.

In addition, there was the important fact that she was Jerry O'Connell's number-one fan in the entire universe. In the multiverse, actually. How many Earths are there, anyway?

The first two seasons were shot primarily in Vancouver.

With the third season, the whole kit and kaboodle was moved to Hollywood. Very convenient for this book project.

Vanessa and I were treated wonderfully. Jerry invited Vanessa to sit on the couch next to him while we did the Q & A. Cleavant played us some cool jazz. John was expansive and funny and showed us his lap-top. And it's impossible not to fall in love with Sabrina (who'd recently had a birthday in her trailer—the party atmosphere was still there).

These interviews appear in their entirety at the conclusion of the book, along with an interview with Tracy Tormé, who had us over to his office later that afternoon where the hospitality continued to flow. Later, I interviewed co-creator Robert K. Weiss, and he helped fill in more of the history.

Imagine a world where this episode guide doesn't include any personal stuff. How sad it would be not to see behind the scenes and find out what's really important. Like the fact that Sabrina Lloyd died her hair red for the third season because they didn't want four dark-haired characters. Or that John Rhys-Davies is a talented writer as well as being a big-time movie star. Or that with his Broadway background, Cleavant Derricks has a talent for music to match the Crying Man. Or that in person, Jerry O'Connell isn't merely tall... but really, really tall.

All four have a natural empathy that is the core of why this show became so popular. In real life, the chemistry is still there... because no one is a good enough actor to fake it.

They are really cool.

PART THREE:
FIRST SEASON

"What if you could find brand new worlds right here on Earth where anything's possible? Same planet—different dimension."

"I've found the gateway!" Sliiiiiiiiiderrrrrrrssssssssssssssssss

So much thought went into the design of the early episodes that it is a cryin' shame (to coin a phrase) that much of that effort was wasted. The original episodes were shot in a different order than they were actually broadcast.

THE ORDER AS FILMED:
1. Pilot (2 parts)
2. Summer of Love
3. Prince of Wails
4. Fever
5. Last Days
6. The Weaker Sex
7. Eggheads
8. The King is Back
9. Luck of the Draw

THE ORDER AS BROADCAST:
1. Pilot
2. Fever
3. Last Days
4. Prince of Wails
5. Summer of Love
6. Eggheads

7. The Weaker Sex
8. The King is Back
9. Luck of the Draw

The first time Fox ran the series in repeat, they changed the order again.

THE ORDER IN REPEATS:

1. Pilot
2. Fever
3. The King is Back
4. Last Days
5. Eggheads
6. The Weaker Sex
7. Summer of Love
8. Prince of Wails
9. Luck of the Draw

Hey, what if you could find a brand new world right here on Earth where the first season order was . . . different? A fourth list. A fifth! Speaking of which, I think I'll have a drink.

As everyone knows, there is nothing quite so dangerous as television trivia. The significance of these lists is that the stories were designed in a logical sequence that is muddled when the order is shifted. I am reviewing/summarizing in the order broadcast, but when there is confusion I will remind the reader how the program was originally intended to be viewed.

There's a lot to say about the first season and the pilot. Along with the cleverness of the situation and the sound dramatic sense in developing the characters, Tormé and Weiss showed political courage. Believe it or not, it took guts to portray a Soviet-occupied

America. All previous attempts at this have received critical derision. There's a fine old Hollywood tradition that the highest standard is a double standard. Many old B films with an unbelievable Nazi scheme are given better reviews and a higher rating in film review books than identical B films with an unbelievable Commie scheme.

In other words, if you show a jackboot kicking someone in the face, and put a swastika on that boot, you generally receive a more positive critical response than if you show the same boot with a hammer and sickle. By electing to portray a Soviet-occupied America, the creators of *Sliders* ran the risk of being accused of McCarthyism. So I knew from the start that *Sliders* would not be a typical TV series.

In his interview, Cleavant Derricks observes that all four Sliders are natural individualists. They represent the best in the American character. They look out for each other while never giving up any of the qualities that make each one special. They are natural-born enemies of any dictatorship—regardless of the symbol a tyrant may choose to write large on the pages of history.

The Sliders are heroes.

The series began like this:

PILOT
Part One

Teleplay by Tracy Tormé
Story by Tracy Tormé and Robert K. Weiss
Directed by Andy Tennant
Music by Dennis McCarthy

GUEST STARRING:

Linda Henning as Mrs. Mallory
Joseph A. Wapner as Commissar Wapner
Doug Llewelyn as Comrade Llewelyn
Garwin Sanford as Doc

FEATURING:

Roger R. Cross as Wilkins
Yee Jee Tso as Wing
Frank C. Turner as Crazy Kenny
Gary Jones as Michael Hurley
John Novak as Ross J. Kelley/Interrogator
Don MacKay as Artie Field
Alex Bruhanski as Pavel Kurlienko
Jay Brazeau as KGB Colonel
Andrew Kavadas as Vendor
Spook Yin Lee as Pal
Wayne Cox as PBS Spokesman
Raoul Ganee as Sentry
Tom Butler as Michael Mallory
Jason Gaffney as Conrad Bennish, Jr.

In a San Francisco basement, a young genius named Quinn Mallory fails to invent an anti-gravity device. He's not disappointed over his lack of success because he has inadvertently come up with a gateway between worlds, a wormhole in the space-time continuum. He keeps this discovery a secret from his widowed mother, who worries that her son is too much like his father, who was such an absent-minded professor that one day he walked in front of a car.

Quinn keeps a videotape record of the gateway's appearances: a shimmering vortex of blue light. It looks like a tunnel. He experiments by sending objects through, ultimately using a basketball with a timer that returns the ball after twenty minutes.

There's at least one person Quinn is certain will appreciate this discovery: his college professor, Maximillian Arturo, who teaches relativistic quantum physics. The question is when and how to break the news. He wonders about this as he walks his usual route through Golden Gate Park, past the Lincoln statue, where a homeless old man rants and raves in outmoded Marxist rhetoric.

Once in Arturo's classroom, Quinn falls into an all-too-usual habit of daydreaming. This does not escape Arturo's attention. Quinn is so close to his breakthrough that it is very difficult for him to concentrate on anything else. At least he never has to worry about coming off as the most spaced-out student while Conrad Bennish (Arturo's favorite target—a metal-head physics student) is also in the class.

Not even Bennish alters the situation. Today is Quinn's day to play space cadet. When he shows up for his job at a computer store, his friend, Wade Welles, notices that something is different. As smart as she's pretty, she has a crush on Quinn but he's oblivious. Today he's beyond oblivious.

By the time he leaves the store, he's decided to take a trip into the wormhole. All the way home, he argues with himself. He can't let anyone go in his place in case something goes wrong. He's not about to risk Schrodinger, the family cat. He can't send a camera because the electrical field would disrupt the recording.

He makes a video recording of preparations for the first manned mission. He dates it and adds a personal note, asking his mother to forgive him if he never returns; and also asking her not to throw out his stuff in case he takes a long, long time to return.

If everything works according to plan, he will be back within a quarter of an hour. He opens the gateway, takes a deep breath and dives in . . . only to be ceremoniously dumped back in his basement.

Convinced that he's failed, he gets in his car and begins driving. At first he doesn't pay much attention to the disc jockey on the car radio who is saying some very strange things. When Quinn almost causes an accident by running a green light, he knows that something is seriously wrong. Then he really listens to the radio. There's a lot more off kilter in this dimension than the reversal of red and green traffic lights. He's on an alternate Earth where vinyl LP's have replaced CD's; where Jack Kennedy is married to Marilyn Monroe and thinking of passing up a second term in the White House; where Americans are crossing the border into Mexico for better jobs . . . and, finally, where Elvis is still alive and performing.

He heads back to his house—the analog of his house in this world. The front gate always squeaked before. Now it's silent. Then he sees his mother. She's married to the man who was the gardener when he left. His elation at having crossed to a parallel Earth receives final verification when the time runs out and, with a surge of energy, the gateway appears and pulls him home again.

Crazy with excitement, he embraces the familiar—everything from his mother to the old creaking gate. Then he rushes off to the university. Now is the time to talk to Professor Arturo. Unfortunately, the professor is not ready to talk to him. Arturo berates him and leaves the classroom. Other students inform Quinn that a short time before, he had attacked the professor's theories, and insulted the man. Even Bennish was blown away by how Quinn dumped on the venerable prof. All this is news to poor Quinn.

Quinn checks out the work place next, which means seeing not only seeing Wade again but also their annoying boss, one Michael Hurley, the classic middle-management type. Wade suggests he get out of there fast. Seems that a short time ago, Quinn told off Hurley. Wade especially likes the fact that Quinn found time to give her a passionate kiss.

Along about this point, our hero begins figuring out what the audience already has a lock on. Messing around with the universe (or multiverse) may have something to do with the latest mystery. He returns to his basement lab and finds . . . himself waiting there.

This other Quinn gives him a present: a few improvements on the blackboard where Quinn #1 does equations. Quinn #2 says that they are both Sliders (his term for inter-dimensional travel) and the more experienced Quinn is on his eighth slide. All questions of Arturo and Hurley aside, this other Quinn sure has some good ideas about Wade.

Quinn #2 is a bit of a braggart. He's been married for two years but doesn't tell the identity of his wife. Before time runs out on this slide, he tells his other self about a world where the Cubs won three straight World Series. He also mentions a virtual Utopia where there is no pollution, crime or hate, or fear. He was the only unhappy person there because he'd set his timer for only twenty hours.

This leads to a discussion of the timing device built into the gizmo that actually opens the gateway. Quinn #2 tries to warn Quinn #1 about something regarding the timer but before he can finish, his time is up. He is sucked out of Earth Prime. His last words suggest that the setting on the timer should not be altered for returning to one's own world.

While Quinn is trying to assimilate all that has happened in one day, he is visited by Professor Arturo and Wade. They are both concerned about his erratic behavior, and the professor wants to give his student a chance to apologize. (The humorous pomposity of

John Rhys-Davies helps set the tone for the series right from the start.)

When Quinn's mother shows them the basement, their world(s) is changed forever. Wade is thrilled and calls the place the Batcave. The professor enjoys a bigger thrill when he examines Quinn's blackboard, on which is now written a proof of the Unified Field Theory.

Quinn joins the party. The good professor does not believe his brilliant pupil has actually opened a doorway between universes until Quinn shows him the gateway. The special-effects people are to be commended. John Allison did the original effects, and co-producer Robert K. Weiss helped develop their look. When it comes to science fiction, the effects always matter. John Rhys-Davies and Sabrina Lloyd capture the sense of wonder with their stunned expressions. But it wouldn't be the same without that spinning, twirling, always-changing effect.

Quinn convinces Arturo and Wade to go on a trip with him.

As he has never taken three people before he boosts the power, not only drawing all three in at the same time but leading to unforeseen consequences.

Driving down the street in a big red Cadillac, passing right in front of the Mallory house, is Rembrandt Brown. He is an R&B singer, the Crying Man, on the comeback trail. Tonight he is scheduled to sing the Star Spangled Banner at a Giants game. He hopes this will help launch him big as a solo act. His previous career was strictly Motown—he was the lead singer of the Spinning Topps. He is thinking about gold records and spinning platters as a large, blue circle moves in front of his Caddy and takes him right off the charts...

Brown's auto crashes into a wall of ice, part of an iceberg covering San Francisco on the alternate Earth where Quinn, Arturo, and Wade have popped into the basement of this other Mallory house, which is every bit as frozen and abandoned as the rest of the buildings. They find a photograph of the Mallory family with a sister Quinn never had on Earth Prime.

When the three inside the house check outside, they find the singer. Quinn tries to explain to the understandably upset motorist just what the hell happened. Rembrandt takes it remarkably well, considering he didn't volunteer for this. But we see that in addition to being frightened, this guy is smart and adaptable—a prerequisite for sliding.

As they huddle in Brown's car, Quinn tells them how much longer they must wait in this wasteland if he doesn't alter the timer portion of the gizmo that triggers the vortex. Brown naturally wants to leave right away in the wild hope that he can still make his gig, but Quinn explains why he considers it risky to alter the timer. During this first meeting, the Crying Man tags Quinn with a highly appropriate nick-name: Q-ball.

Their discussion is quickly brought to an end by the intrusion of a gigantic cyclone bearing down on them. They have no choice but to leave right away or die. Quinn creates a new gateway directly over the roof of the car. They must enter it one at a time as the tornado grows closer every icy second. Arturo goes first, followed by Wade and then Rembrandt. Quinn slips and falls back into the car as he sees the opening begin to contract.

Meanwhile, the professor lands on green grass . . . on a nice warm day, and turns over just in time for Wade to land on him.

She doesn't weigh much and he makes a nice cushion. Plus there's an interesting exchange of expressions that I hoped might lead to something. They move out of the way before Rembrandt alights on the same patch of grass.

Wade is the first to express concern over what's keeping Quinn.

When she insists that they must go back for him, Arturo explains the full implications of sliding—and that if Quinn didn't make it through they may very well never see him again.

As this sinks in, Wade realizes how much she truly loves Quinn. Right before the gateway closes, our hero plummets through. He notices how happy they are to see him but remains oblivious over how much happier Wade is than the others.

They recognize that they are in Central Park in San Francisco. Still hoping to get to the stadium on time, Rembrandt hails a taxi. He doesn't give it a second thought that he's been picked up by a Russian cabdriver.

Wade doesn't give it much thought that the phone booth she enters is labeled PTT instead of ATT. Not until she fails to give the proper identification number, and is instructed to stay where she is until the security police show up, does she realize that something is seriously wrong. As she steps outside the booth, she sees the lettering: PEOPLE'S TELEPHONE AND TELEGRAPH.

Quinn and Arturo discover they are not in their world when they notice one significant discrepancy in the park. The statue of Abraham Lincoln is no longer a statue of Abraham Lincoln. In its place stands a statue of Vladimir Ilich Ulyanov, with the more famous pseudonym Lenin underneath. Below that is a brief statement honoring the greatest revolutionary leader of the twentieth century. This tribute is in perfect English.

The Sliders realize they have really slid into it this time. They can't leave until the timer recharges itself, which could happen soon...or never.

Wade rejoins her friends and warns them that the phone company is after her. (I love stuff like that.) They go in search of Rembrandt but it's not going to be easy. The cab could have taken him anywhere. The trio find more evidence of an America gone topsy-turvy. The bum from the park is now a candidate for the Senate.

Meanwhile, Rembrandt fails to communicate to the cab driver

that he's expected to sing the anthem at the Giants game. When the driver turns on the radio, there is an anthem playing. Rembrandt has never heard it before. Along about now, the Crying Man starts to get the general idea, especially when he tries to pay the toll with a dollar bill. Half a dozen soldiers appear and hold Kalashnikov rifles on the unhappy singer, inspiring the best line of the episode:

"Do you need exact change?"

PILOT
Part Two

Teleplay by Tracy Tormé
Story by Tracy Tormé and Robert K. Weiss
Directed by Andy Tennant
Music by Dennis McCarthy

GUEST STARRING:

Linda Henning as Mrs. Mallory
Joseph A. Wapner as Commissar Wapner
Doug Llewelyn as Comrade Llewelyn
Garwin Sanford as Doc

FEATURING:

Roger R. Cross as Wilkins
Yee Jee Tso as Wing
Frank C. Turner as Crazy Kenny
Gary Jones as Michael Hurley
John Novak as Ross J. Kelley/Interrogator
Don MacKay as Artie Field
Alex Bruhanski as Pavel Kurlienko
Jay Brazeau as KGB Colonel
Andrew Kavadas as Vendor
Sook Yin Lee as Pal
Wayne Cox as PBS Spokesman
Raoul Ganee as Sentry
Tom Butler as Michael Mallory

The political aspect of what happens next was already covered in the introduction. Tracy Tormé elaborates on why they chose a Soviet America in his interview: "It was kind of like Jack Webb's nightmare of America."

The Crying Man is taken to an interrogation center in a converted warehouse. There he is turned over to the tender mercies of a man who was a shyster lawyer back home. This establishes a nifty trend on *Sliders*, namely recurring characters between worlds. Rembrandt's taxi driver, Pavel Kurlienko, will appear on other Earths. We

have already seen the lawyer on Earth Prime as Ross J. Kelley, complete with hokey TV ad. Now Rembrandt listens to the same insincere promises from the lips of an interrogator.

We learn that the Rembrandt Brown of this world died twelve years earlier in a Detroit uprising. Kelley suggests to his superiors that the man in custody took the identity of the real Mr. Brown and must be part of the revolutionary underground because only they use the old, banned U.S.A. currency, a trademark of the resistance. The Crying Man has plenty to cry about when he is informed that he will receive justice on *The People's Court*.

Back on the streets, Arturo has better luck than Rembrandt when the professor tries to pass a greenback. The hot-dog vendor who receives the money is himself a member of the revolution. Just then, the phone police zero in on Wade and her friends. The vendor leads Arturo, Quinn, and Wade to safety in underground headquarters that are literally under the ground—beneath the city streets.

The revolutionaries are more than happy to see Wade, especially a black officer named Wilkins who kisses her. Hard. (She's been getting kissed a lot lately.) In this world, Wade is commander of the revolution as well as being Wilkins' lover. The revolutionaries are less pleased to see Maximillian Arturo because on this parallel Earth he is citizen general of the People's Army, Western Sector. Arturo's life is only spared because he is in the company of Wade, and even so he is subjected to indignities.

Wade finally convinces the rebels that she and her friends are from an alternate America where Joe McCarthy was there to save us from the Red Terror. (Just kidding!) Anyway, she convinces them that Things Are Not Always What They Seem. Wilkins verifies that his Wade is still being held in the prison run by General Arturo. The revolutionaries realize they have a potential godsend in the timely arrival of these doppelgangers.

When Quinn and Arturo are released, thanks to Wade, our heroes are given a crash course in how the United States fell to the forces of international Communism. The Sino-Soviet Empire is where things started going to hell. The United States lost the Korean War. Russian and Chinese cooperation ended in the economic isolation of the United States from the rest of the world, culminating in actual occupation by the Soviets.

While the visitors from Earth Prime are being treated to this historical horror show, one of the privates who looks a lot like Michael Hurley tunes in a popular television program, *The People's Court*. As chance would have it, Rembrandt is being brought before this Marxist-Leninist version of Judge Wapner's TV courtroom. This is a bit more serious than the average small claims case, however, as the Crying Man is given plenty of reason to weep: a fifteen-year sentence in the Alaskan Gulag.

The good news is that Rembrandt will be held in the same facility where Commander Wade is being held before they ship her to Moscow for public execution. The revolutionaries have not managed a raid because they lacked a plan to get past heavy security. All this has changed now that the citizen general is with them. If the timing is on their side, Arturo is sure he can pull it off.

Outfitted in the uniforms of the security forces, and heavily armed, the bogus general's special troops move their convoy to the federal penitentiary. At the gate they encounter a brief problem with a guard, but Arturo passes the identity check with a hand-scan. He is, after all, himself!

Arturo and Quinn rescue Rembrandt. Wade is looking for the other Wade in another wing of the prison when the alarm goes off. The guard has received the unbelievable information that the general is at home in bed.

The good guys shoot their way out past the bad guys, and the skirmish ends with Wilkins' firing a bazooka. As they escape, Wade is shot as she sits next to Quinn. At the first opportunity, they pull off to the side of the road where medical attention is given to Wade. Too late. They're losing her.

As Quinn weeps over his loss, Wade comes up behind him and sees how hard he is taking the fact of her death. It is, of course, Commander Wade who is dying; and it is Wilkins who must face a world without Wade. Quinn and Wade embrace as the young genius promises that somehow, some way, he will get her home. He'll never be as oblivious about Wade again.

Professor Arturo and Quinn work together on the timer/gizmo. Wade tells Wilkins and the others about the Earth she knows. The freedom fighters are fascinated to hear the story of the Berlin Wall coming down. The collapse of the Soviet Union in our world gives them hope to carry on the fight in theirs.

Rembrandt Brown sings over the bodies of Commander Wade and her fallen comrades. This affords Cleavant Derricks the opportunity to do a gorgeous rendition of "Amazing Grace."

The Sliders prepare to slide with no idea if they will reach home or another parallel Earth. Their best bet is to return to the park where they arrived. On the way, they run afoul of a curfew and open the gateway right before a mob of angry pursuers reaches them.

When they depart, they are looking at the statue of Lenin. When they arrive, they are looking at the statue of Lincoln.

They think they're home.

Everything seems the same. Rembrandt has a nervous moment when Pavel, the same Russian taxi driver, picks them up; but this version of the driver recognizes Rembrandt as the pop star the Crying Man. That's good enough to convince the singer that he's home.

Quinn needs more convincing. After he checks the front gate at his house and it squeaks, he's more comfortable. He invites everyone inside. His mother seems the same. She makes Quinn and his friends a nice dinner.

The Sliders are in the middle of a discussion about the advisability of taking more trips to alternate Earths when the front door opens and a distinguished looking man joins the party. He is Quinn's father. Quinn's late father....

Apparently, the Sliders are only beginning their long journey.

The last line of my novel reads: "When Thomas Wolfe wrote that you could never go home again, he didn't know about Sliding."

FEVER

Written by Ann Powell and Rose Schacht
Directed by Mario Azzopardi
Music by Mark Mothersbaugh

GUEST STARRING:

Ken Pogue as Dr. Morton
Allison Hossack as Dr. Eileen Stanley

WITH:

Yee Jee Tso as Wing
Alex Bruhanski as Pavel Kurlienko
Marie Stillin as Waitress
William Sasso as Gomez Calhoun
Dean Haglund as Stock Boy
David L. Gordon as Tactical Moonsuit
William MacDonald as Medical Moonsuit
James Bell as Trucker
James Timmins as Pharmacist
Gavin Cross as The Sick Man

Following the pilot is always a tough act. So the second slide should have avoided a scenario in which our heroes enter a tyrannical world and quickly ally themselves with the local underground. We just saw that. It was a piece of good fortune that the Wade of Commie World was a significant player in the revolution. Now we move into "dumb luck" country, where Quinn is a significant player in the revolution of this world.

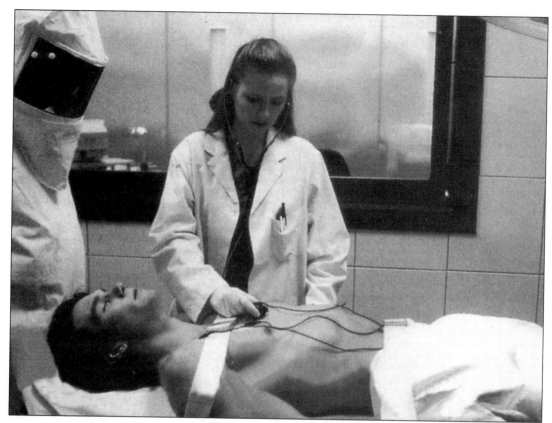

In defense of this episode, we should check out the list for the order in which the stories were filmed. Originally this would be have been broadcast fourth, a much better placement. My research assistant, Vanessa, also observes that this is the first episode in which Jerry O'Connell removes his shirt, so that counts for something.

At least this one starts out with an entertaining teaser showing us something brand new. They're in a world where everyone around them is hitting it rich in oil. Quinn's house on James Street struck a gusher in his backyard. They have eleven seconds to enjoy this before the next slide.

Things are not as good in the next world. A huge white truck spraying a mist into the air almost runs down Wade when a man dashes out of the shadows and rescues her. Instinctively, she kisses him in thanks . . . but the guy freaks out, horrified at the physical contact, and runs off.

Other clues that they've entered a medical nightmare are: plastic-wrapped, sterile hamburgers with almost no flavor as the only bill of fare in a restaurant; everyone dressed shabbily and trying to avoid physical contact; the fear caused by anyone who coughs; and, finally, a police state run by the California Health Commission. The capper is that in a restroom, Rembrandt notices a wanted poster for Public Enemy No. 1, Patient Zero, who happens to be this world's version of Quinn Mallory.

Any thought of simply holding up and waiting for the next slide is blasted when Wade becomes sick—probably as a consequence of her lips coming in contact with her rescuer's cheek. The storm troopers in biochemical warfare suits begin hunting our Quinn when a waitress ID's him. Then a crazy hotel clerk almost blows Quinn away. Talk about lousy service. . . .

Arturo keeps his head and points out that they don't dare bring this plague with them to the next world.

They learn this is a dimension in which Pasteur never discovered penicillin. Quinn #2 was a medical student who allowed himself to be experimented on. He was infected with a virus fatal to everyone else although he is immune. When the scientists get their hands on our Quinn, they can't understand how Patient Zero tests out as not having the "Q" infection. Wade, delirious and near death, stumbles onto the underground. Arturo and Rembrandt follow her, and they are all taken by the rebels.

She meets her first other Quinn (as he met his first other Wade in Commie World). This Quinn is also brilliant. Arturo convinces him of the reality of sliding. The immediate problem is to save Wade who has all the symptoms of Q disease—sore throat, high fever, hallucinations, red eyes—before she reaches the most annoying symptom of all: death.

During this sequence, Arturo and Rembrandt learn the horrifying truth that antibiotics don't exist in this world. Other bad news: when the virus first began to spread, the government created healthy zones for the rich. The underclass is under a death sentence for Q disease.

With Wade's life hanging in the balance, Arturo attempts to grow some cultures with which to make penicillin. By now, the professor and the Crying Man realize they have contracted the disease as well. Rembrandt decides the time has come to rescue Quinn from the bad guys.

Quinn escapes in good James Bond fashion. He finds a biohazard suit that actually fits his long and lanky frame. The climax reunites the Sliders. Arturo takes a test dosage of his penicillin. He survives. They give it to Wade. She survives. They may now slide with a good conscience because they won't be infecting a new world.

In the few minutes remaining, they also inspire Quinn #2 to achieve a complete social revolution, withholding the new antibiotics until rich people realize that poor people are just like them . . . or something. As if in editorial comment, the Sliders next enter a world of cannibals, where people are just like lunch.

LAST DAYS

Written by Dan Lane
Directed by Michael Keusch
Music by Mark Mothersbaugh

GUEST STARRING:

Jason Gaffney as Conrad Bennish, Jr.
Jennifer Hetrick as Caroline Fontaine
George Touliatos as Dr. Lee Antonovich

WITH:

Gerry Nairn as Mace Moon
Malcolm Stewart as Alan Fontaine
Carlton Watson as Reverend
Robin Palmer as Nurse Pamela
Patrick Stevenson as Jimmy
Hidalgo Rubin as Driver
Jacqueline Dandenaeu as Metermaid
Norma Wick as News Anchor
Brian Arnold as Science Correspondent
Mike Dobson as Policeman

This episode combines a nuclear scenario along with planetary ping pong. Once again, it manages to be politically incorrect. This time the forbidden thought is that there may be occasions when it is useful to possess a thermonuclear device.

"Last Days" starts out in the world of the main storyline.

Rembrandt is first to notice that there's a lot of kissing going on.

Wade picks up on the party atmosphere and teases Quinn about the last time he kissed someone.

Good feelings don't last long when they begin noticing weird stuff: corporate executives hanging out with Hell's Angels, stores guarded by security guards with machine guns, seventeen-dollar apples next to items priced in the pennies.

Then they see a sign: FINAL DAYS SALE. A man tears up his parking ticket right in front of a meter maid, indicating that the end of the world is near.

The impending apocalypse be-comes personal as the Sliders dis-cover that their next window of opportunity won't be until after zero hour. (Their lack of control over when they slide was explained in the earlier-filmed "Summer of Love," which, thanks to the change of broadcast sequence, led to some in-teresting theorizing among Sliders fans this first season.)

The script by Dan Lane takes full advantage of the dramatic possibili-ties. The Sliders don't know if this version of San Francisco contains analogs of family and loved ones, but Wade and Quinn try to find out in case this world is the end of the line. Everyone agrees to re-unite before Asteroid 2956 collides with the Western Hemisphere on Friday at 5:00 P.M., two days after their arrival. They are scheduled to stay three days.

While Quinn and Wade hunt for family members, Rembrandt goes off by himself. He finds a group of people partying and sings for them, saves a woman from a fatal round of Russian roulette, and ends up working in a church soup kitchen. Arturo devotes his remaining time to understanding how this threat has come to pass and wondering if there is anything to be done.

The professor attends a seminar of the Union of Concerned Scientists and encounters this world's version of Conrad Bennish, more zoned out than ever. Bennish is unceremoniously escorted out of the auditorium for insisting that they must develop an atomic bomb. Arturo lets it sink in that he's in a 1990s world without any nuclear option. He makes contact with Bennish, who doesn't know any Arturo on this Earth. They form an immediate partnership: two men with two days to come up with a functional atomic bomb if the world is to be saved.

Of course, Arturo quickly figures out that on this Earth, Einstein lied about the possibilities of nuclear fission so as to spare the world the threat of nuclear war. We must also assume a world in which Einstein and his colleagues were not as afraid of Adolf Hitler and the possibility of Nazi victory—a strong concern in the letter Einstein sent to FDR suggesting that such a bomb could be developed. On his own, Bennish figured out that in the original testing the detonator was deliberately misaligned. He's dedicated his life to this research and has access to the prototype.

Back on the home front, Wade is unable to find her family so she joins Quinn, who doesn't fare much better. His mom has left to join her parents but this leaves the house for Quinn, and the key is under the mat. They discover sliding equipment in the basement, but this alternate Quinn made a different discovery, leading him into genuine time travel instead of crossing between parallel dimensions. Under the time constraints, there's simply no way of converting the sliding equipment for their purposes. Worse, Quinn accidentally fries the electronics, thus closing off even the avenue of a time-travel escape.

As impending death becomes real to them, Quinn and Wade pay more attention to each other. They make dinner, dance, express their feelings . . . and begin a process of sliding with which more of us are familiar. No sooner do they kiss than Arturo—with perfect timing—bursts into the room and reminds us in the audience that we are watching a television show and not an R-rated movie. (It must be admitted that Fox has been making progress in this area.) Arturo needs Quinn's help with calculations that can help save the world.

Arturo and Bennish have actually finished the bomb, but not without a heavy cost. The good professor had to listen to Metallica until he could stand it no longer, and then Bennish thoughtfully switched to AC/DC. Bennish is so wacked out that Arturo questions leaving knowledge of the atomic bomb in his hands. While Bennish is using the bathroom, Arturo erases crucial information from the diagram.

Quinn adds his brain power to the project. The bomb will be launched at the asteroid by a missile. Suddenly the Union of Concerned Scientists actually cooperates (the one fantasy element of the show).

A good old ICBM missile delivers the warhead and it works. Bennish is the hero of the world. On a more personal note, Rembrandt rejoins the others when they were beginning to think he may have had enough of them.

The Sliders celebrate the salvation of a world and slide on to new adventures. In my favorite moment of the show, crazy Bennish is shown to be smarter than Arturo thought he was. The metal head still has the formula for the atomic bomb and reassures us all with, "Anyone messes with us now—BOOM!"

PRINCE OF WAILS

Written by Lee Goldberg and William Rabkin
Directed by Felix Alcala
Music by Mark Mothersbaugh

GUEST STARRING:

Ben Bode as Prince Harold
Sherman Howard as Hendrick
Liz Sheridan as Miss Miller
Kathleen Duborg as Rebecca
Gary Jones as Michael Hurley

CO-STARRING:

Gerard Plunkett as Driver
Chris Humpheys as Raider #1

WITH:

Tracey Olson as Dixon Vallely
Bernie Coulson as Raider #2
David Kaye as Reporter #1
Jaylene Hamilton as Reporter #2

One of the funniest episodes posits a world in which the colonies settled their quarrel with King George in an amicable fashion. Apparently the only way for twentieth-century Americans to suffer anglophobia is to keep them under the thumb of the British monarchy. This episode provided a wonderful opportunity for John Rhys-Davies to devour the scenery as the sheriff of San Francisco.

The show begins with our heroes atop the Transamerica building, the only structure in San Francisco above water level after the giant tidal wave engulfs it in an episode we haven't seen yet! If the series had been broadcast in the order the shows were made, the opening of "Prince of Wails" would be a great payoff for the cliffhanger that ended "Summer of Love" at the conclusion of which they were deposited at a spot near the tallest building. You'd certainly want to be near a tall building if on the horizon there's the tallest tidal wave this side of Noah's Flood. Maybe the power was left on in  the deserted city so they could take the elevator to the roof. Maybe they had just enough time to climb all those stairs. Whatever they did, it's a fair solution to a cliffhanger.

All of this cleverness was wasted because the powers-that-be changed the broadcast order. Anyhow, our heroes are struggling not to fall in the drink when they see what they think is a shark—but it's a far more horrific monster—circling them. We can imagine how happy they are to slide even though the wormhole takes them to the British States of America.

They start off on the right foot, oddly enough, when Wade is almost run over by a car (shades of "Fever"). Will those crazy drivers please watch out for that girl? The driver acts as though he's almost committed a horrible crime, instantly proving this is not a San Francisco with which we are familiar. This is a San Francisco where they honor the British Express Card.

The driver's solicitude turns out to be less a product of a higher order of civilization than typical human nature. In this world, Arturo is a powerful and dangerous man. The driver realizes that he almost whacked someone in the Arturo party and he wants to make amends. He works for the Royal Colony Hotel. The four are given the Royal Suite. This is where they learn that this Earth's Arturo is acting regent of the Western Americas—until the rightful heir, Prince Harold, can be crowned. The alternate history lesson: in 1779, George Washington was executed along with other revolutionaries.

They head for the hills. Hiding out in the countryside might have worked this time if their car hadn't broken down. And who should they bump into but Prince Harold himself.

Harold isn't alone. He's surrounded by the sheriff's men, who are about to slay him on the spot. It's very handy that Arturo looks like . . . Arturo! The soldiers obey his orders to cease and desist. He sends them back to the city. The tables are turned as a band of renegades calling themselves the Oakland Raiders (no comment at great length) capture the Sliders and Prince Harold.

Thinking quickly, Quinn announces that he, Wade, and Rembrandt wish to join to revolution. As a sign of good faith, they have brought the sheriff (Arturo) and the prince as prisoners. The revolutionaries can't believe their good fortune, and well they shouldn't. When they ask for a ransom, the real Sheriff Arturo is unmoved. He has no reason to pay ransom for himself. Besides, he wants the prince dead, as the behavior of his men strongly suggests. With Harold out of the way, Arturo is next in line for the throne.

Sheriff Arturo orders his men into the woods, a show of force that hardens the hearts of Professor Arturo's captors. Quinn must save Arturo and Prince Harold from execution, which he does with a delightful speech combining quotes from Robin Hood, FDR, old adages, JFK, the Bible, the Black Panthers, and a reversed saying of Mao Tse Tung. The revolutionaries are overwhelmed by the power of Quinn's non-sequiturs. They spare Arturo and Harold. After all, Quinn brought them the captives in the first place.

A nice sub-plot involves Wade and the prince. He starts to fall for her, or at least so it seems. She likes him enough to untie him. He rewards her gesture by promptly escaping.

Quinn follows Prince Harold and is captured by the sheriff's men. This world's Arturo is a hard case. He plans to execute Quinn on public television as an object lesson to recalcitrant Yanks. He doesn't reckon on the plans of our Arturo, who hatches a scheme to rescue Quinn. He is aided in this by the prince, who rejoins the revolutionaries. Apparently his highness has started noticing what goes on around him.

The plan is elegant in its simplicity. The Oakland Raiders simply occupy the television station and broadcast a signal so powerful that the authorities can't keep it off the air. Instead of the sheriff's prime-time sadism, the home audience is treated to a speech by Prince Harold, who relieves this world's Arturo of authority. He then gives a speech heavily influenced by our heroes.

Goldberg and Rabkin have a lot of fun with the Sliders' stepping into the role of the Founding Fathers. Quinn gets out of the electric chair before the juice is turned on. Wade turns down an offer to marry the prince and become queen of the reformed nation. Rebecca, the female leader of the Raiders, kisses Quinn passionately right before the slide. Small wonder that she was ready to start a terrorist campaign to either rescue Quinn or avenge his memory.

No one seems to appreciate what a great deal Americans have in this world. As Sheriff Arturo points out during one of his cozy television chats, subjects of the crown only have to pay 74 percent of their income in taxes. If we ever reach a 74 percent rate in the United States, what do you want to bet there won't be a revolution? Only bad militia people would want that.

SUMMER OF LOVE

Written by Tracy Tormé
Directed by Mario Azzopardi
Music by Mark Mothersbaugh

GUEST STARRING:
Deborah Lacey as Sharon Brown
Arther Reggie III as Arther Reggie III
Jason Gaffney as Conrad Bennish Jr.

CO-STARRING:
Gerry Nairn as Mace Moon
Michele Goodger as Copeland

WITH:
Robert Lee as Harold Yenn
Barry Pepper as Skid
Ajay Karah as Seeker
Richard Leacock as Tremelo
Gabrielle Miller as Fling
Joy Coghill as Mrs. Tweak
Mike Dobson as First Policeman
Joanna Piros as Newscaster

I'm the guy who misses both the Do-Your-Own-Thing counter culture sixties and the Reagan decade of greed-and-materialism. The combination of them is my idea of heaven. Instead I'm stuck in the nineties, the decade of guilt and regret, the decade of endless whining about zero tolerance of nearly everything. I wish to hell I could slide out of here and never look back.

"Summer of Love" is an important episode for me because it addresses these feelings, providing an alternate history in which the

sixties experience might have happened in the nineties. Those of us who lived through that period realized it didn't end until well into the seventies, with the conclusion of the Vietnam War and Nixon's leaving office. For science fiction, the late sixties and early seventies was a time of experimentation.

Yes, it was a damned good party. Twenty years later we should have had another party at the end of the Cold War, celebrating the fact that we won and didn't go up in mushroom clouds. At the successful conclusion of World War II, Americans knew how to party. Now we whimper.

Like I say, I needed "Summer of Love," and it's one of my favorite episodes. This was an especially good episode for fans of Sabrina Lloyd, a group in which I count myself at the head of the line.

The episode begins with the FBI interrogating our old pal Conrad Bennish. Despite their lack of scientific background, the FBI wants him to explain the sliding machine. While this peculiar scenario is playing out, the Sliders enter a San Francisco where they can't find any people. They're not lonely for long. This dimension offers thousands of creatures fresh from a Venezuelan lab and flying in their direction: half spider, half wasp . . . and all monster.

Now remember, this episode was to have come directly after the pilot, which means they shouldn't have any trouble sliding out of here whenever they want. They obviously resumed their travels when Quinn's father turned up alive (proving that they weren't home yet). Around about now, they probably wish they'd stayed put but there's no cause for alarm yet.

To create suspense, the timer/gizmo begins smoking and making worrisome noises when Quinn fires it up. The vortex forms but more slowly than usual . . . and the device begins emitting black smoke. The gateway finishes forming in the nick of time, just as the droning of the swarm makes it abundantly clear that the monsters have arrived.

Wade and Rembrandt make it through but then the gate sputters shut. This allows the special-effects people to show off their stuff, John Rhys-Davies to show real frustration, and Jerry O'Connell to convince us yet again that half the battle is not to panic. The wormhole opens again, allowing Arturo and Quinn to reach the same San Francisco as Wade and Rembrandt, but in a different location within the city.

They enter a world where Ollie North is president and the United States is fighting a war in Australia. The enemy is Japan because the Pacific war was not resolved here. (Imagine the Outback Kong!) The counter-culture has emerged thirty years later than it did in our history.

Now the fun begins. Wade and Rembrandt are welcomed as prophets by a commune. Sliding always makes for an effective entrance. While Wade grooves on the situation, Rembrandt borrows a car from the commune. These guys have bread!

Rembrandt sets out to find Quinn and Arturo. En route, he checks out his old house and walks in on a wake being held for the Rembrandt of this world, who is MIA in Australia and presumed dead. Back home, Rembrandt had a thing for a woman named Sharon but never followed through. In this world, he married her. The idyll ends badly the next day when Rembrandt finds out that, as a wife, Sharon is a harridan who expects obsequious behavior from her hubby. He makes a run for it.

Quinn and Arturo rent a second-story loft where they can work on repairing the timer/gizmo. Unfortunately, their landlady, Mrs.

Tweak, is a person just like her name (a nice performance by Joy Coghill). She's one of those psychotic law-and-order types who rarely exist outside the pages of the underground comix we used to buy at head shops. She telephones the FBI informant line and suggests that her tenants be put under surveillance. Part of the joy of this sequence is Arturo's being mistaken for a subversive hippie. His new threads make him look like Professor PETER MAXimillian.

Back at the commune, Wade is really getting into the role of a guru. It's not every day you meet a lot of new friends who see you arrive via special effects.

She introduces her followers to something completely new: astrology. This may be the wildest diversion from our history when one remembers that astrology is thousands of years old. Or has the repressive Establishment managed to keep mysticism out of the hands, and heads, of the young?

Weirdest moment: in answer to a question about where the universe ends, our girl answers that it's just beyond Mars. We're never told what she's been smoking. There's one bittersweet moment when the humor stops. A boy named Fling asks if the Summer of Love will go on forever. Sabrina Lloyd captures the right tone and a perfect expression as she pauses and then softly tells the desperately desired lie. "Yes. It's true."

Quinn and Arturo are having considerably less fun. Diminishing funds reduce their meals to peanut butter and crackers. They're making progress on the equations, though, without which they'll never repair the gizmo. With the perfect timing fans have come to expect, Quinn finishes repairing the device just before the apartment is invaded by the FBI.

Just then, Quinn looks out the window and notices Rembrandt driving by. The plot unthickens. Arturo grabs one of the agent's guns. He and Quinn beat it out of there. They chase down Rembrandt.

All three go to the commune where Wade is still holding court, recommending nonviolent resistance to the war but also counseling draft resistance. She makes her case very effectively even though Arturo questions her meddling in this world's affairs without knowing more about its history. She counters that she is not his student and that there are certain universal truths.

Now we get to the point in the script where they lay the new ground rules for sliding, and it's worth repeating Quinn's crucial statement: "There will be a single window of opportunity on each Earth we visit. A moment in time when the weakened powers of the gizmo will still allow us to access the gate. We're lucky we didn't miss the window on this world."

Speaking of which, they slide to a San Francisco about to be engulfed by the giant tidal wave.

"Prince of Wails," anyone?

EGGHEADS

Teleplay by Scott Smith Miller
Story by Scott Smith Miller and Jacob Epstein
Directed by Timothy Bond
Music by Mark Mothersbaugh

GUEST STARRING:
Charles Cyphers
Peter Spellos as Jimmy Fountain
Gabrielle Rose as Kristina Fox Arturo

SPECIAL GUEST APPEARANCES BY:
Rick Garcia as Referee
Tom Jackson as Color Commentator
Ron Pitts as Play-by-Play Announcer

CO-STARRING:
Andrew Guy as Wilson
Karen Austin as Lydia
William B. Davis as Professor Myman

FEATURING:
Roman Danylo as Boyer
Johnny Mah as Victor
Rachel Hayward as Karen
Anthony Harrison as Agent Cannon
Marc Baur as Agent O'Malley
Sheelah Megill as Mrs. Dana Bingham
Colin Warner as Harvard Captain

Bentley Mitchum as M.I.T. Player
Mark Poyser as Rapper Leader
Carl Hibbert as Rapper #1
Michael McMillian as Rapper #2
Amanda O'Leary as Librarian

In the world of "Eggheads," intellectual achievement is valued the way we honor athletic prowess. The most popular sport is called "Mindgame."

Here's another story in which the Sliders start off in the dimension where the main action will take place. The first clue that they're not home is when they see a bus-stop poster proclaiming: ALBERT EINSTEIN WORE KHAKIS.

Then there's the teenager with a boom box blaring out the heavy chords of Tchaikovsky. The capper is a huge Nike-ad-style poster like the ones they put on the side of buildings. The one they see doesn't feature Charles Barkley or Michael Jordan. This one features Quinn Mallory typing on a notebook computer. The caption reads: JUST THINK IT.

Suddenly Quinn is recognized. While a crowd swarms around him the way teenage girls gather around Jerry O'Connell, the regular viewer of the show anticipates that we're in a world where its version of Quinn recently slid out of there, leaving an interesting opening for our Quinn. The same assumption applies to Arturo when it is discovered that he, too, is a celebrity on this Earth. Smart as they are, Rembrandt and Wade are not Mensa members, apparently, and one weakness of this episode is that more wasn't found for them to do.

Arturo easily slips into the role vacated by his doppelganger: chairman of the university. Quinn's other Quinn is world famous as a top player in "Mindgame," a team sport that combines physical exertion with the intellectual rigor of science and math questions. A sexier version of a college quiz show.

The biggest surprise is that this is a San Francisco where the public knows both Quinn and Arturo as Sliders. The rascals made a production out of the adventuresome manner of their departure, drawing parallels between themselves and great explorers of his-

tory (which they certainly are, regardless of motives). The point is that they needed to slide because the Quinn and Arturo of this world did some naughty things.

Our heroes deduce that where there is sliding there must be a sliding machine capable of taking them home. The first stop is Quinn's house. Alas, a bank foreclosure has beaten them to the punch. No lab. No equipment.

Next, they check out the possibility of sliding equip-

ment at the university. Arturo's office provides this episode with another nice gag, a poster of the good prof playing Las Vegas on the Algebraic Variations Tour. They don't find the sliding machine but Quinn's college teammates find him.

The captain of the team is back and now the UCal Eggheads have a chance against the Harvard Crimson. The contest will take place at the Mindfield at Berkeley.

A nice subplot develops when Arturo finds out he's being sued for divorce by the woman who, in his world, he truly loved but lost to a brain hemorrhage. He tries to make amends but to no avail. Turns out that his double doubled up with too many co-eds. John Rhys-Davies turns in some fine acting in the scenes with his estranged wife.

This episode's irony quotient is supplied by Rembrandt betting against Quinn, a not-unreasonable move considering Q-ball's initial performance in a game with which he is unfamiliar. The rules require the player to run with a ball while answering highly technical questions; the player captures a square with each correct answer. Rembrandt's error is in forgetting what a quick learner Quinn is.

Although Quinn does badly at first, he wins the game with a spectacular play before the clock runs out. So Rembrandt loses the Sliders bankroll. Well, at least they're in a world whose money is the same as back home. Rembrandt won't get into trouble for passing counterfeit bills.

Suddenly the story takes a turn into suspense country. Danger arrives in the character of Jimmy Fountain (played by character actor Peter Spellos), who passes on the information that Quinn owes a cool million dollars. No wonder the guy needed to slide. The gangster's philosophy is that a Quinn in the hand is worth however many in the vortex. He explains the situation with helpful kicks to the ribs and philosophical musings about cognitive dissonance. The upshot is that Fountain wants M.I.T. to win the finals. If Quinn throws the game, the million-dollar debt is paid.

Quinn cannot bring himself to throw a game even when he can slide away from the consequences. He also didn't enjoy Jimmy's free rib massage. He goes to the coach and tells the man he won't play.

The FBI shows up with a grocery list of felonies committed by Quinn's double. He makes a deal with the feds, trying to make amends for the other Quinn.

Ditto for Arturo, who is busy trying to clean up some of the mess left by his double. He tape-records a message to his double on the expectation that the accident that befell our heroes probably didn't happen to these other Sliders, who will probably come home. Arturo lays down the law to Arturo. He tells how devastated he was when his Christina died, a message that would strike the conscience of anyone not spiritually dead.

The climax is action packed. Quinn puts his team so far ahead that all they have to do to win is keep one player out, a man Quinn has learned is on the take. Jimmy the gangster thinks all this demonstrates a very bad attitude. The bad guys chase the good guys. The FBI chases the bad guys. Everything comes to a head on a rooftop where the wormhole opens up to the consternation of Jimmy, and it's on to new adventures.

THE WEAKER SEX

Written by Dawn Prestwich and Nicole Yorkin
Directed by Vern Gillum
Music by Mark Mothersbaugh

GUEST STARRING:

Sara Botsford as Mayor Anita Ross
Robert Curtis-Brown
Jill Teed as Serena Braxton

CO-STARRING

Alf Humpheys as Pete
Andrew Wheeler as Ken
Liza Huget as Lois
Peter Kelamis as Glenn
Douglas Sills as Ed
Joe Maffei as Bernie
Teresa Barnwell as Hillary Clinton
Tamara Stanners as Jeanie Moses
Leigh Morrow as Anchor Woman
Peg Christopherson as Female Shopper

"The Weaker Sex" should receive high marks for what it tried to do.

At first the Sliders think they're home when they arrive in Golden Gate Park. A moment of sheer horror dissuades them. It tops anything by Stephen King or Clive Barker. They see President Hillary Clinton addressing the nation on television. Since only a sexually insecure male could be bothered by America's strongest and smartest woman's assuming her proper station, one more piece of evidence is required to prove that the Sliders have entered Hell: the spectacle of Jane Pauley as Pope.

Anyway, our intrepid heroes (and heroine!) learn that in this world women grew weary of seeing their menfolk go off to war. Reversing thousands of years of human history, these gals decided to carry the sanctity of life to such ludicrous extremes as to prohibit wholesale slaughter. After the peace-mongers took over it was only a matter of time before men could no longer be trusted in positions of authority. In this view, testosterone is more dangerous than menopause. Well, this is science fiction.

The Sliders must spend six and a half weeks in Hillary's Village. One of the realistic aspects of the series is that when they spend a significant chunk of time somewhere they get jobs. Less realistic is that they succeed in this without sinking in a bureaucratic swamp of proving their identities, or else they easily slip into roles vacated by their doubles.

Rembrandt's experience is my favorite of this episode. He adapts more quickly than the others to the exigencies of the situation. He begins singing on the streets and collects enough lucre to pay for a hotel room and food for the group. (I always approve of any script that gives Derricks a chance to sing.) He continues his street gig until he is picked up by a stylish woman in an equally stylish Porsche. Her name is Serena. This incredible babe promises to hook him up with some record producers if he'll put out for her.

This is a good episode.

Anyway, Rembrandt gives in to temptation. Neither is really hurt. Is that so wrong? Of course, it must be admitted that she didn't treat him as well as she might have. She uses men. How shocking.

The dialogue sparkles throughout "The Weaker Sex." Wade takes a high-ranking job on the woman mayor's reelection campaign. Gone is the nonjudgmental guru of "Summer of Love."

Arturo is so annoyed with the situation that he runs for the office of mayor, even though he's only a man. What a trouble maker. He finds a politician buried deep in that massive chest of his and speaks out for all the disenfranchised boys of this mad, sad world.

As the campaign heats up, Quinn raises the issue on everyone's mind. What will Arturo do if he wins? Miss the slide? From Arturo's point of view, Quinn isn't helping matters when he takes a job as a receptionist in the mayor's office. Quinn wins back the professor's good will when he resigns from the mayor's campaign over a TV ad run to smear Arturo.

After an attempt is made on Arturo's life, Wade has a change of heart and questions the wisdom of the Sliders' involving themselves in this world's politics. Sooner or later, the Sliders always put personal loyalty and friendship ahead of ideology. One more reason why the show is slammed from both the conventional left and right.

A different kind of politics reaches a head when Rembrandt is caught in Serena's apartment by her ex-boyfriend. The Other Man confesses that she's not really a record promoter. Rembrandt confronts the lady and leaves just in time to attend the debate between Rembrandt and Mayor Ross.

Concerned about the impending slide, and not wanting to hurt the cause of men by winning and then vanishing, Arturo decides to guarantee his defeat by pulling a Mondale. He has an emotional breakdown in front of the cameras. Quite predictably, his tears achieve the opposite effect. In what lock-step feminists would condemn as the most sexist moment of the show, a man's tears melt the collective female heart. With any luck, the human race can get back to warfare sometime soon.

However, the bounce in the polls isn't sufficient to make Arturo a winner. He concedes. The Sliders slide.

Epilogue: Turns out the exit polls were wrong. Arturo won after all. If only he knew this. While still in Hillary World, he made a bet with Wade about the election that if he lost, he must be her slave for the next nine days, five hours and thirty-five minutes—the time they spend in the next world.

There are, one imagines, worse fates.

THE KING IS BACK

Written by Tracy Tormé
Directed by Vern Gillum
Music by Mark Mothersbaugh

GUEST STARRING:

Chuck McCann as Captain Jack Brim
Clinton Derricks-Carroll as Alternate Rembrandt
Tom Pickett as Maurice Fish

SPECIAL GUEST APPEARANCE BY:

Eadie Del Rubio, Elena Del Rubio & Milly Del Rubio
    as the Del Rubio Sisters

CO-STARRING:

Janet Kent as Lawyer
Michelle T. Carter as Penny Jensen
Sheri-D Wilson as secretary

FEATURING:

William Sasso as Gomez Calhoun
Judith Maxie as Charmange
Nicholas Harrison as Nick
Peter Hanlon as Expert Analyzer
Richard Ihara as Judge
Tyler Van Blankenstein as First Kid

For fans who were starting to miss the teaser openings, this one starts off with a bang. They are in a California where Quinn is about to be sentenced to death for the crime of graffiti. For spray-painting an overpass, the sentence is death by lethal injection. Quinn proclaims his innocence but his words fall on deaf ears in the courtroom. The implication is that in this world, his double is a cold-blooded graffiti-path.

Well, how can anyone possibly expect justice in an America where the most popular '50s TV sitcom was *I Love Ethel*?

Proposition 199, the "Instant Justice Initiative," was passed in this California, so Quinn is about to be murdered—oops, I mean legally executed—ah, what the hell, murdered. Fortunately, the slide is only eleven seconds away.

Arturo forms the gateway right in the courtroom. Quinn is wearing handcuffs but fortunately no leg irons. He breaks away from the bailiffs and dives into the vortex. The others follow, leaving behind yet another society more demented than our own.

They plop down on the floor of the same courtroom in the next world over. This place of justice is superior in one important respect: it's empty. They quickly exit the courtroom before acquainting themselves with this society's taboos, traditions, laws, common law, policies, statutes, habits, or community standards.

Right away Rembrandt discovers that this is a much-improved society. The good news is that there's a Crying Man convention in San Francisco and Rembrandt Brown is "the undisputed king of rock-'n-roll." The bad news is that they only have three days in this paradise.

The Sliders check into a hotel. That's when they learn this convention is being held to celebrate the eight-year anniversary of Rembrandt's death. This prepares us for every Elvis-sighting joke ever told, presented in alphabetical order. The convention is a showcase for Rembrandt look-alikes from all over the country. They must be showing some of his movies, too, featuring lots of surfing and girls in bikinis.

Cleavant Derricks carries the show, and sings some real gems. A fan has caught our Rembrandt on tape and the word is out that the Crying Man is alive. Another nice gag is that Quinn and Arturo were captured on the same video tape and mistaken for Jim Morrison and Luciano Pavarotti. So what I want to know is why no one mistakes Wade for a musical sensation?

Rembrandt shoulders the awesome responsibility of being as big as Elvis. He ventures outside the hotel to meet his fans, an ever-growing mob of well-wishers. Only trouble is that they wish him so much goodness that they almost rip him apart in the excitement. Arturo (who must beat off a few of his fans as well) has to save him.

Enter Captain Jack Brim, the man who was Rembrandt's manager here, or so he says. The captain offers Rembrandt the opportunity of doing a worldwide TV comeback special. The price tag will be one million dollars a song. Wonder what Quinn thinks of that when they were in so much trouble in the world of "Mindgame" just because he owed a lousy million.

No way the Crying Man is gonna turn this down! His friends think he should let the offer slide. For one thing, the timing is bad. The night of the big concert is the evening of the slide. But Rembrandt is not to be swayed when the dream of a lifetime is about to come true.

A plot complication is that Maurice Fish, a former member of the Spinning Topps, in this world is crazy enough to be a record producer. He kidnaps Rembrandt. Quinn happens to get the license plate and, despite uncooperative police (who quite reasonably assume it is a publicity stunt), tracks down Fish on his own.

Meanwhile, the Rembrandt of this world cannot fail to pick up on all the free publicity. Faking his death was the only way he could think to retire and enjoy his privacy. With all the news coming down, he can't stay out of it. He enters Captain Jack's office as the remaining three Sliders exit. (A scene worthy of the Marx Brothers.) He tells Jack that Maurice is a total psycho he had committed years ago.

As if to drive home the point, the Sliders break into the Fish house in the nick of time. The disgruntled Topp was about to slit Rembrandt's throat.

The high point of this episode is when Rembrandt meets Rembrandt, with twin brothers performing the roles. The alternate Rembrandt is willing for our Rembrandt to take his place and perform the comeback concert. Rembrandt still can't say no. His alternate will stay and listen to the music because he wants to make sure his replacement has what it takes.

His friends don't want to lose him but they realize the power of the dream that has come between them. Rembrandt takes the stage. Wade informs the other Rembrandt of the million-dollar-a-song deal. Alternate Rembrandt takes the stage and picks up the song in midverse, surprising our Rembrandt so much that he just stops. This world's Rembrandt comes over to our Mr. R., and tells the crowd to give a hand for the greatest Rembrandt impersonator of all.

Which pretty much solves the problem seven minutes before the slide. My favorite line in this episode is from Rembrandt 2: "They built a shrine to me in Memphis called Crying Land."

LUCK OF THE DRAW

Written by Jon Povill
Directed by Les Landau
Music by Dennis McCarthy
Theme by Mark Mothersbaugh

GUEST STARRING:

Nicholas Lea as Ryan
Cynthia "Alex" Datcher as Julianne Murphy
Kevin Cooney as Ken Neisser

SPECIAL GUEST APPEARANCE BY:

Geoff Edwards as Himself

CO-STARRING:

Tim Henry as Agent Jones

WITH:

Mike Kopsa as Agent Wilson
Nathan Venering as Father Fergus
Walter March as Fatherly Man
Kristina Matisic as News Anchor
Ted Cole as Friendly Man
David Glyn-Jones as Elderly Man

This is my choice for the most politically incorrect episode of all. By positing a world with a lottery that encourages people to commit suicide in return for a brief moment's pleasure, a scenario is created in which Catholic priests and those of like mind are protesting for the right to life in a context in which no one can criticize them. In the 1990s, no other program has dared to offer an image remotely like this.

Of course, this is a darkly satirical portrayal. So much rage is expended over the abortion debate today that it overshadows the impending euthanasia debate of tomorrow. The lottery is about the latter. Ultimately, the courage of this episode doesn't lie in any position taken about the right to live, right to choose, right to die, or any other particular. It is really about how mass media sets the terms of the debate.

"The Lottery" begins in the world of the main action. Wade observes that everyone looks content. Right away we know this spells T-R-O-U-B-L-E. Everything is quaint, including the cobblestone streets. Another bad sign is revealed when Rembrandt notices the low prices on consumer goods (which I don't think would be possible without a growing economy, but never mind).

When Arturo loses his wallet, it is promptly returned by a gracious citizen. In *Sliders*, that's cause for paranoia. Then the Sliders find something that should make them eager for the next slide: ATM machines that give out money whether or not you have an account. You receive money by playing the lottery.

The rules of the lottery are simple. The more cash you take out the better your chance of winning. The prize is five million dollars and a white credit card that all merchants must honor for unlimited purchases. The lottery receives the address of players the moment they play. The Sliders are staying at a motel.

Arturo's natural conservatism serves him well, and saves him. He plays but takes no more cash than the small amount he sees the locals take. He withdraws one hundred dollars. Rembrandt is more daring. He withdraws five thousand dollars. Wade proves herself unacquainted with the Austrian school of economics and withdraws a lot more. She's gambling on this San Francisco's being as utopian as it first appears. Quinn passes.

Back at the motel, Quinn finds a copy of *Time* magazine and learns that there are only 500 million people on the planet. The population of San Francisco is less than 100,000.

Wade asks Quinn to go horseback riding with her, affording another opportunity for them to explore their feelings for each other. In the first season, the romantic potential seemed to be going somewhere. She suggests they should consider staying here in a calm, languid, peaceful world. Her best argument is that the timer/gizmo might give out one of these days and they could be stuck somewhere horrible.

The motel is not far from a lake, and Rembrandt persuades Arturo to join him on a little fishing expedition. While the Sliders are enjoying this idyll, the episode's dark humor surfaces with an announcement from a TV news anchor about President Jocelyn Elders' attending the dedication of the reopening of the Thomas Malthus Center for Sexual Ethics and Education. This society seems very serious about population control.

The lottery results are announced that evening on television while the blissful quartet enjoys trout amandine (the day's catch). There are twelve winners and Wade is second on the list. Rembrandt didn't make it.

The next day consists of limousines, jewels, flattery, fine dresses and fine wine, and accumulations of wealth without corresponding obligations. Or so it seems. Rembrandt comes along for the ride and meets a gorgeous woman named Julian, another of the winners. He is smitten with her. This romantic event occurs at a fashion show where the female winners are being shown the Paris fall collection.

The festivities are a bit much for Quinn, who exits in search of fresh air. Wade is upset that he's upset. She chases after him, and he admits that he's afraid of losing her to this world.

Like a modern-day Odysseus, Quinn will keep sliding until he finds home, even if he must finish the journey alone. Despite what has come between them, Quinn agrees to meet Wade at the lottery winners' dinner that evening.

When Quinn doesn't show at the prearranged time, Arturo escorts Wade to the dinner, where she meets another winner named Ryan. The young man and Wade hit it off and spend the rest of the evening dancing. Rembrandt and Julian do likewise. The visitors from our Earth do not pick up on the subtle vibes that they're partying on the Titanic. They're falling into the typical pattern that says lots of money means you settle down, mate, and reproduce.

Reproduce? This world seems extremely concerned over the subject of reproduction.

Quinn finally enters the scene wearing his characteristic we-have-a-serious-problem expression. He finds Arturo and shows him a pamphlet he was given by a right-to-life group picketing outside the hotel. The lottery is part of the population-control system. The winners eat, drink, and make merry...because tomorrow they die.

A minor criticism: if the lottery winners are going to die at dawn after the big dinner, they didn't begin to have enough time to spend millions of dollars or even put a dent in the white card. Even if they are allowed to leave all these goodies to loved ones, it still seems a cheat if they don't have at least a few months to try and spend all that money.

Once Wade and Rembrandt are told the truth, the remainder of the story would be the usual race against the clock to make the next slide. Except with this being the season closer, they wanted to do something special.

Rembrandt tries to convince Julian to come with him to another world. Wade makes a similar attempt with Ryan by also telling him the truth.

To his horror, Rembrandt is turned over to the lottery police—potentially a fate worse than death because in this Zero Population Growth utopia the authorities torture anyone who interferes with the lottery! Perversely, Julian doesn't think she's betraying her lover. She believes the story about Sliding must be a delusion and she extracts a promise from the authorities that they won't torture Rembrandt for trying to escape—a promise that's good just as long as she lives, of course. After she's gone, the gestapo will take him to the Municipal Processing Center, where he will learn about another way of dying.

Time for Quinn and Arturo to do a rescue mission again. Wade goes into hiding to await their hopeful return. The lottery officials find her and it looks bad, but she has a temporary reprieve when Ryan comes to her rescue and knocks out the constabulary. In a bit worthy of James Bond, Ryan turns a fire extinguisher into a useful weapon.

Then there's the omnipresent good-luck factor. Quinn and Arturo encounter a picket line of right-to-lifers in front of the processing center who are overwrought about the tortures and murders going on inside. With criminal disregard for government property, the protesters get in the way of the van taking Rembrandt to his fate. Quinn helps stir up the crowd so effectively that the authorities fear an incident.

"Stop the slaughter!" declaims the priest. A nice touch. The protesters swarm the vehicle and begin rocking it, trying to tip it over. Quinn smashes the windows and opens the door to let Rembrandt out of the back of the van.

Police show up but the Sliders slide through the crowd in all the confusion. A smoke bomb helps. They commandeer a public vehicle that runs on electricity. Security safeguards shut down the car but Quinn breaks into the fusebox and gets the wheels turning again.

The Sliders are reunited back at the swank hotel. Wade is still with Ryan as the vortex comes into view. All five make the slide, but Quinn picks up a bullet in the back from an over-zealous cop. When they reach the next world, Ryan is amazed at the miracle, but not for long. Something more serious has happened.

The last shot is of Wade weeping, cradling the bleeding Quinn in her arms.

END OF FIRST SEASON

PART FOUR:
SECOND SEASON

"What if you could travel to parallel worlds? The same year, the same Earth, only different dimensions?"

"A world where the Russians rule America, or where your dreams of being a superstar came true, or where San Francisco was a maximum security prison?"

"My friends and I have found the gateway. Now the problem is finding a way back home!"

SLIIIIIIIIIIIIIIIIIIDEEEEEERRRRRRRSSSSSSSSSSS

INTO THE MYSTIC

Written by Tracy Tormé
Directed by Richard Compton
Music by Anthony Marinelli
New Theme by Anthony Marinelli and Stephen Graziano

GUEST STARS:

Christopher Neame as Dr. Xang
Phil Fondacaro as Bounty Hunter
Hrothgar Mathews as Mr. Gale
Nicholas Lea as Ryan

WITH:

Mikal Dughi as Nurse
John Novak as Ross J. Kelley
Alex Bruhanski as Pavel Kurlienko
Karin Konoval as Fortune Teller
Rod Wilson as Sorcerer
Deanne Henry as Mrs. Mallory

When fans tuned in for the start of the second season, the kind of world the Sliders had just entered was less important than the fate of Quinn Mallory. If a touch of magic was needed to save our hero, none of us expected a visit to the Wizard of Oz. But first we had to follow the yellow brick road...

The story begins in a rural cemetery. A tombstone reads: QUINN MALLORY 1974–1996—BORN ON A DISTANT SHORT, DIED ON AN ALIEN WORLD.

This is a bad sign. Wade stands next to Ryan. Another bad sign. Arturo speaks the eulogy. Rembrandt doesn't sing "Amazing Grace."

A weird undertaker watches their every move. Wade announces her intention to stay on this world with Ryan. She paints a grim picture of domestic bliss that means the death knell for future adventures.

Just when it looks as if *Sliders* is about to be transformed into a family sit-com, Quinn wakes up from his nightmare. A good sign.

The reality is that Ryan did ask Wade to stay with him but she turned him down. As if to tell fans they shouldn't resent the guy who they only imagined was a threat to our hero, the script reveals that Ryan removed the bullet from Quinn's shoulder.

Less impressive is how the problem of the Other Man is resolved. He simply departs, making it easy to forget him and slide to the next world.

Right before they slide, Quinn notices a sinister farmer watching them. It's the same man who was the undertaker in the dream. Hrothgar Mathews has one of those distinctive character-actor faces that enrich horror films. Quinn is eager to get away from him.

Sliding right after the extraction of a bullet is probably not the best idea. Of course, they don't have a choice. Quinn hurts his arm upon landing. The timer shows that they'll be in the new place long enough for him to seek medical attention. The first doctor they find is Dr. Xang.

The diplomas on the office wall are for doctorates in Auric and Pranic Healing. The cosmic hole through which they travel has brought them to the land of holistic healing. Even the eye chart is the version with the witchcraft alphabet. Biased in favor of Western allopathic medicine, they don't consider the hocus pocus worth the $266.00 fee. Besides, it's more than they've got. This time they don't slide out of trouble. They split.

The doctor sues Quinn for "retribution substitution," a Shylock-ian procedure wherein the plaintiff is allowed to take a portion of the defendant's anatomy in payment. There must be something about Quinn that spells high intelligence wherever he goes because the doc wants nothing less than the poor boy's brain.

A world of dark magic must have its fair share of lawyers. They find one who has no trouble believing in sliding because a most important citizen is known to be a Slider, the aptly named Sorcerer. The lawyer advises them to make the dangerous trip across the Golden Gargoyle Gate Bridge to the wizard's castle . . .

Well, the writers carried the Oz parallels only so far. Quinn already has brains but someone is trying to take them away, a reversal of the Scarecrow's situation. Wade stands in for Dorothy, the girl who wants to go home. Rembrandt already has a heart . . . and courage. Arturo already has courage . . . and a heart.

Of course, crossing the bridge can't be much worse than the night they spend in the Dominion Hotel. For all the occasions they will spend in this specific hotel in various dimensions, it is never more appropriately named than here in a world of magical domination. Service comes complete with baying wolves outside, clanking chains in the hallway, and a grim reaper figure at the doorway (he delivers subpoenas here).

Pavel, the taxi driver, is back, and takes them to the bridge. Arturo and Wade engage in an interesting debate during the taxi trip. Arturo seems to realize that he's in a science fiction series and argues bravely on the side of scientific orthodoxy. He insists there must be a logical (i.e., non-magical) explanation for what they see around them. Wade takes the other side, convinced they have entered a world of true magic.

In the debate between science and superstition, Quinn keeps out of it, the good engineer who combines both practicality and imagination. I wish he'd quoted Arthur C. Clarke's famous observation that a sufficiently advanced science is indistinguishable from magic.

The Golden Gargoyle Gate Bridge provides even more creepy fun than the hotel: bats, owls, creepy laughter, and an invisible portion of the bridge. A sign reads: WARNING! THIS BRIDGE IS CURSED! CROSSING IT IS HAZARDOUS TO YOUR HEALTH! All that's missing is the Cowardly Lion assuring the night that "I do believe in spooks."

They make it across and it isn't the castle of the wicked witch. Inside, however, there is a marked resemblance to a certain Emerald City. The challenge is to get inside. They are met by the Sorcerer's Apprentice—er, assistant: a Mr. Gayle, who happens to be the same creepy fellow who was the undertaker.

For generations of kids, one of the most frightening moments in movies was when Judy Garland and her friends first met the giant floating head that is the Wizard of Oz. Although only an illusion in a world where most of the threats are genuine—including the wicked witch and her minions—the Wizard is far more frightening than any real danger. So when the Sliders encounter a giant monster Sorcerer, all the little-kid voices in the back of our heads remind us to look behind the curtain. In this first encounter, the Sliders don't know where the curtain is.

The task is not to bring back the broom of a witch but to return to the city and steal the plans for a sliding machine from Dr. Xang. On their way back across the bridge, they are stopped by a bounty hunter who takes them to the doctor's office for a purpose of his own. The bounty is for Quinn's brain. The equipment is conveniently provided for removal of said brain. This time Rembrandt saves the day and gets the drop on the bounty hunter.

So, plans in hand, they return to the castle. This time they receive a reception that is missing only musical numbers and the horse of a different color.

They "look behind the curtain." The real Sorcerer turns out to be this world's Quinn. A clever touch. This is a version of what his genius might have accomplished if he'd stayed put instead of gallivanting across the multiverse. Mr. Gayle is the business partner who convinced him that the "magical" empire Quinn built would collapse if the masses knew the truth of the technology behind it.

Finally, the Oz references are turned upside down when this particular wizard says it is within his power to grant their wishes and send them home. He is very convincing.

Following is my favorite scene from the entire series. After the slide, they have only one minute to decide if they are home. Quinn checks the gate and it doesn't squeak. A quick perusal of a newspaper provides the news that the Raiders are playing in Oakland; O.J. Simpson is being tried for a double murder; and the Cleveland Indians are in the World Series. On the strength of this data, they decide this can't be home and slide out of there.

The epilogue consists of Quinn's mother and the gardener's coming out the front door. We learn that he just oiled the gate. The Sliders should have had faith.

LOVE GODS

Written by Tony Blake and Paul Jackson
Directed by John McPherson
Music by Stephen Graziano

GUEST STARS:

Gwynyth Walsh as Detective L. Specateli
Jennifer Nash as Diana
Georgia Emelin as Billie Jean
Jon Pennell as David

WITH:

Deb Podowski as O'Grady
Kathryn Anderson as Jane
Andrew Guy as Trevor Grant
Kendall Cross as Cara
D. Neil Mork as Stationary Biker
Dawn Roberts as TV Newscaster
Jane Knox as Woman #1
Jan Bailey as Woman #2
Ona Grauer as Debra
Kathleen Barr as Aussie Guard
Kamilyn Kaneko as Clerk

This is Jerry O'Connell's favorite episode and it's easy to see why. A world of love-starved women where males are so rare as to be highly valued is the premise of some of the corniest and most fun science fiction ever done in movies or comics.

Judging from magazine covers alone, the decade with the most examples of worlds of love-starved women was the fabulous fifties. In those days, it was believed that women without men had little purpose. Pre-Barbarella society didn't have a lot of imagination, and its technology was deficient in certain significant respects. Women were supoosed to stand around and wait for men to show up. This was understood as a fantasy even then, but in our day and age one scientific expedition to Santa Monica provides some idea of what a

planet of women might do with themselves.

With this valuable background in mind, the Sliders enter a world inhabited by billions of women and only a handful of men. It is also a society that never developed artificial insemination and that can be viewed by kids in family viewing hours. They don't call this science fiction for nothin'.

The Sliders are surrounded by a female mob at Fisherman's Wharf. They are saved by female police officers. When they are interrogated, one question predominates: How did they survive the virus?

The Alternate History Lesson: the usual war-of-the-week in the Middle East became serious for a change. Instead of the fairly impotent power it is in this world, Iraq was a force to be reckoned with. It released a virus that attacks Y chromosomes. Most of the world's men were exterminated. Ironically, all the Iraqi male population died as well.

The super power on Earth is now Australia. Paul Hogan would be so proud. The Aussies were far enough away from the poison cloud that eleven hundred of the men survived. The importance of these

men is made painfully clear by the existence of the Bureau of Repopulation. The race is on between nations to repopulate the globe.
Men have become military assets. They are referred to as "breeders."
Special agents are dispatched to kidnap men for the good of their
country's GNP.

Although Jerry O'Connell really enjoyed this episode, Quinn complains of being graded like a piece of meat. At the repopulation center, men learn that they are expected to breed with six or seven
women per day. The Sliders also learn from a newfound friend,
David, that in this society the love that dares not speak its name is
monogamy.

A clever aspect of the plot is that not all countries are playing this
game. Mexico has no forced breeding. David offers to take the male
Sliders along with him if he and his new wife (who remains free on
the outside) can pull off an escape.

But what about Wade in Woman World? She's free but under surveillance. Naturally she criticizes the nature of things and is informed that not all women go along with this treatment of surviving
males.

David and his wife succeed with the escape plan and take the
male Sliders with them. Quite foolishly, they return to David's
house. Unknowingly, Wade leads the police right to her friends. The
officers from the Bureau of Repopulation are not the only ones after our boys. Further complicating matters is the fact that Australian commandos have found out about the fresh meat and these
ladies want to do the patriotic thing.

At first, all the Sliders escape the dragnet—but David's wife is arrested. Then Arturo is shot with a tranquilizer by the Aussies and
taken by them. Although Quinn takes a shot as well, he manages to
get away when a woman named Jane Hill rescues him and takes him
to her bachelorette pad.

What she wants in return from Quinn is not unreasonable. Her
husband was killed by the virus before they had children. Quinn

could solve her problem in a manner more intimate than the impersonal system of using breeders (and even then, the odds are against any single woman's receiving her turn at bat).

Meanwhile, Arturo finds his captivity in the Australian Consulate even more intolerable than being held by the Bureau. The attitude of the head captor, who talks tough and tells him to eat his vegemite, does not inspire him to put forth his best efforts. He's good and ready to be rescued.

A man can show no greater love than by giving up his dignity for a friend. Picture Rembrandt in drag as part of Wade's rescue plan. Wade and Rembrandt manage to talk their way into the Australian Embassy. When they see Arturo, Wade convinces the Aussies she can get them a stud breeder from the center in exchange for the professor.

Wade promises the Bureau three top-line breeders in trade for David's wife and their star breeder, whom Wade convinces them is about to be sterilized. Her plan works. At the exchange, she creates total chaos. Arturo, Rembrandt, David, and his wife all get away in a van. The only problem is: what about Quinn? He rejoins them just in time for the slide. Quinn has done what he can to help his rescuer become pregnant.

The Sliders exit in characteristic fashion, and David and his wife do their own version of a slide: they go to Mexico.

GILLIAN OF THE SPIRITS

Written by Tony Blake and Paul Jackson
Directed by Paris Barclay
Music by Anthony Marinelli

GUEST STARS:

Deanna Milligan as Gillian
Tom Butler as Michael Mallory
Gillian Barber as Nicole

WITH:

Gerard Plunkett as Father Jerry
Greg Rogers as Major Phillips
William Sasso as Gomez Calhoun
Mitch Kosterman as Muscle Guy No. 1
Peter Fleming as Traffic Policeman
Sheelan Megil as Mrs. Henry
Nicole Parker as Monica
Alex Ferguson as Cab Driver
Sylvio Pollio as Guard No. 1

Through the unheeding many he did move, A splendor among shadows, a bright blot upon this gloomy scene, a Spirit that strove For truth, and like the Preacher found it not.
—Shelley, "Sonnet"

n this episode, the title character sees "ghosts," and her community treats her as a crackpot/harmless eccentric. At least they don't burn her at the stake. No one considers the possibility of phenomena badly observed—that she might be seeing something out of the ordinary that could be explained by a scientific/materialist theory no one has come up with yet. The "ghost" haunting her in this story is no shade of a corpse risen from the grave . . . but a very alive Quinn Mallory caught between dimensions.

The soggy teaser drenches the Sliders in a torrential rain. Quinn is the last to slide out of the deluge just as a random lightning bolt strikes the mouth of the gateway tunnel.

In the next world, Wade, Rembrandt, and Arturo arrive together as the vortex closes behind them. No Quinn! Maybe they slid on Friday the 13th. The lightning has caused a problem.

There's a powerful moment of acting from Sabrina Lloyd. Her emotional explosion matches the storm they just left. Is Quinn her ideal lover, an ideal brother she never had, or something more? Whatever the answer, she hates the thought of living without him.

Sliding without Quinn isn't any fun.

The others don't realize that Quinn has accompanied them, landing a short distance away courtesy of what appears to be a second vortex. When he approaches, they can neither see nor hear him. If he tries to touch them, his hand passes through their bodies. He tries to pick up a rock and his hand passes through it. He is a literal ghost.

He can keep tabs on them. It's a good thing that he follows along because he finds out that they have another problem besides his in-betweenism. The lightning also scorched the timer/gizmo. If they can't fix it in time, they will miss the next window and any hope of going home.

If all this isn't vexing enough, the alternate history of this world presents them with more problems. Written by Tony Blake and Paul Jackson, who would move into co-executive positions, the script throws everything at the Sliders but the kitchen sink. After Hiroshima, Americans were so horrified they effectively banned high technology. This is a wild idea because the reaction in real history was quite the opposite.

How to repair the timer/gizmo in a world without high tech? Sliding is of the space age. Now they find themselves in an America frozen in the late 1940s. Most terrifying of all is that there's no television!!! Makes the blood run cold.

Arturo is almost arrested for wearing a digital watch. The Sliders do what they do best, besides sliding. They make a run for it. Quinn watches, unable to help although it seems that he can "spook" a horse. Rembrandt observes that although high tech is contraband, the authorities know it when they see it, and that means there must be a black market for the stuff. Arturo is impressed with the Crying Man's idea.

The question is how to find the market. Rembrandt has a suggestion. One of them can try to tell the truth to a priest in confession, counting on the man to keep their confidence.

They attend a nearby Catholic church, followed by their "ghost." Quinn has become used to not being noticed. So it is quite a shock to him when a teenage girl at the communion rail actually sees him! She tries to look away but not before he has recognized what's happened. As he walks toward her, she bolts out of the church. Quinn is close on her heels. When he confronts her in the street, she begs him to leave her alone. To any passerby, she's talking to herself or an imaginary companion.

Her name is Gillian. She is played by Deanna Milligan in a performance worthy of early Sandy Dennis. She has had this gift, which she's come to think of as a curse, all her life. She sees people on the astral plane.

Quinn persuades Gillian to write a note and then pass it to his friends. A clever idea. He tells her the white lie that he'll leave her alone if she writes the note. If she's the only person who can communicate with Quinn, there's not much choice about using her.

Gillian takes the note to Wade: "Try not to worry about me. I'm alive and with you now, trapped on the astral plane. I'm hoping we can reunite once we slide out of here.—QUINN"

Quinn keeps after Gillian and communicates more details to the others, including an incident from the episode "Last Days." That helps convince Arturo. Before anything more useful is accomplished, Gillian's mother shows up and spirits the girl away.

Rembrandt sticks to the original plan of speaking to the priest. He goes into the confession booth and tells all. To strengthen his story, he pases the timer/gizmo to the priest through the partition. This is a calculated risk that pays off. The priest doesn't think Rembrandt is pulling a prank, and more importantly, the man is not part of the anti-technology mania. Rembrandt's faith has been rewarded. He's found the right priest to give him direction.

They go to the Mallory house in this world where they meet Mike, Quinn's father. His Quinn died from polio. Arturo angrily observes that the death is a consequence of restricted technology.

Mike Mallory spent five years in jail for working with electrical components. He still has quite a collection of boards and tubes that he's willing to share with his other-dimensional visitors.

Something very important is established that seems to be forgotten in the third season. It has to do with the distinctions the show has made between Arturo's more theoretical approach and Quinn's hands-on inventing. Arturo becomes impatient when he can't repair the timer/gizmo.

To top off the professor's frustration, Mallory's basement is raided by the feds and the timer is confiscated. Quick talking by Mike saves the Sliders from being arrested. Or so it seems.

Meanwhile, Quinn is not leaving Gillian alone. She remains his only hope of communication with his friends. She has a job at a coffee shop where the other girls enjoy tormenting her. But not this time. The most annoying of the girls steals money from Gillian's register while she's arguing with Quinn, which seems to be her latest bout of fantasizing. Quinn uses his ability to move through things to see the stolen cash in the girl's purse. This gets Gillian off the hook with her boss, and allows her to take off the rest of the day to help our heroes . . . if she can avoid her mother, that is.

Quinn follows the men who stole the timer/gizmo from his father's house and tracks them to the Bayside Power & Electric Company. In the bowels of this gray building, the inventor of sliding receives a more tremendous shock than any lightning bolt can provide. His father is collaborating with the bad guys. They're smart bad guys, though, busy stockpiling high tech and working on new inventions in anticipation of the day when the anti-technology laws are repealed by Congress. Although Mike doesn't believe the story about sliding, he can tell high tech from BS, and the timer/gizmo is plenty real. The plan is to drain our heroes of their technical knowledge and then do away with them.

Thanks to Gillian, Quinn is able to pass on the grim information to his friends. Arturo and Rembrandt sneak into the facility and recover all the pieces of the timer/gizmo, and grab a few extra components that might come in useful. This workroom has a lot of useful stuff in it.

Back at the Mallory house, Arturo does a much better job of engineering this time. Quinn guides him, through Gillian. Quinn's dad surprises them, gun in hand, but is unable to stop the experiment because he can't make himself into the bad guy he's working so hard to become. Besides, it turns out that he was let out of prison early only if he'd play ball with the boys at Bayside P&E.

Mike Mallory has an epiphany when he sees his dead son materialize in front of the wormhole. Outlined in the radiant energy of the vortex, Quinn becomes visible to everyone, and Gillian is finally proven sane. Rembrandt, Arturo, and Wade slide—after emotional farewells to Quinn. He can't slide with them because the gateway they are using is not on the astral plane. Considering how he first arrived in this world, he should be expecting what the wormhole does next.

He can slide when the gateway passes through the astral plane.

Gillian and Quinn bid each other a touching farewell, and he takes a last look at his father before he leaves to rejoin his friends. The problem that never occurs to anyone is that if Quinn is out of synch here, and he is traveling in the astral plane, might he not remain there forever, always a "ghost" following behind the others? A Flying Dutchman of parallel Earths!

THE GOOD, THE BAD, AND THE WEALTHY

Written by Scott Miller
Directed by Oscar L. Costo
Music by Anthony Marinelli

GUEST STARS:

Karen Witter as Priscilla
Jamie Denton as Jack Bullock
Kent Faulcon as Billy Rae
Keegan MacIntosh as Jamie

WITH:

Peter Lacroix as the Sheriff
Lochlyn Munro as Billy the Kid (originally intended
    to be Billy "The Kid" Gates)
Stephen Fanning as Cliff Sutter
Greg Thirloway as Hank Arnette
Barry Levy as Jed Dalton
Adrian Hughes as Deputy Joe Bob
Bark Anderson as Lonnie Skayler
Roger Barnes as Exchange Official
Jackson Cole as Poker Player
April Telek as Honey Sue
Dean Allan Hinckey as Crooner

This tale of gun totin' legal sharpshooters begins when the Sliders gratefully enter the world of the main storyline. Judging from the condition of their clothes, they have departed a place unusually challenging to their survival skills. They are sandy, sunburned, and parched.

A little boy, dressed as a cowboy, witnesses the arrival. He is so impressed that he stops playing with his cap gun long enough to stare. He asks how they did it. Quinn says they're magicians. The boy, whose name is Jamie, is impressed and directs them to the nearest restaurant, the Wall Street Saloon.

This timeline is a gem. The Republic of Texas under Sam Houston refused to join the United States. While the North and South engaged in the late unpleasantness, Texas went its own way and expanded all the way to the Pacific. The ultimate result of this geo-political revolution is that Rembrandt gets a menu where every dinner on it includes steak, which is just fine with him. For variety, there's armadillo fajitas.

An Armani-clad bully by the name of Jed Dalton is harassing a smaller man and knocks him down. When a fine lady named Priscilla tries to stop him, he pushes her away. This riles Quinn. He steps into the fray and before he can say "Einstein-Rosen-Podolsky Bridge," he's challenged to a duel to the death.

Dalton counts to three. Rather than dying, Quinn actually picks up the gun and fires. The other man drops dead. Quinn is surprised at the outcome. He is not someone who regularly practices at the shooting range. The man who just died is obviously experienced in the use of firearms.

In San Francisco, Texas, gun-toting lawyers are the negotiators who settle legal issues with hot lead. The Code of the West supersedes institutionalized law. Quinn is now a celebrity for having taken out Dalton, who was considered the top negotiator. All silver linings come equipped with clouds. Quinn is taken into custody by the sheriff, who doesn't seem enamored by the code but is hamstrung by cultural tradition anyway.

The sheriff's discomfort is easy to understand when one cool dude, Billy Ray from Drexel-Bullock (the law firm where Dalton worked), walks into the police station and insists that Quinn be turned over to him. The lawman reluctantly agrees. Things look bad from Quinn's point of view. He figures he's headed down his last trail, but the sheriff knows how the system works and is reluctant to let another hot-shot killer escape punishment.

Sure enough, when Billy Ray takes Quinn to the lavish offices of the company, Quinn is in for a surprise. Jack Bullock himself offers him a job. Seems that anyone good enough to outdraw Dalton is expected to fill the vacant position . . . if he knows what's good for him.

Quinn hems and haws in exactly the manner of someone looking for the best possible deal. To help sweeten the offer, Billy Ray takes Quinn to a nearby saloon where the best legal talent hangs out. This scene inspired my law professor friend, Butler Shaffer, to comment, "This gives a whole new meaning to bellying up at the bar."

Billy Ray and Quinn swig a lot of beer together. Suddenly another tetchy lawyer challenges Q-ball. (Rembrandt's nickname for Quinn seems like a good name for a gunslinger.) Billy Ray is so offended by the man's presumption that he steps in for Quinn and blows the sucker away. Quinn pauses to think over how close he's come to death again, and drinks more beer.

Meanwhile, back at the ranch (I had to say that), the others are concerned about Quinn. He finally rejoins them at the good old Dominion Hotel. Wade, Rembrandt, and Arturo see a new side of Quinn. The lad's drunk! There's much entertainment value in seeing

Quinn Mallory flop down on the bed, sloshed, tipsy, sliding without the vortex.

Enter Priscilla with a cure for Quinn's inebriated condition, a can of the dreaded Prairie Oyster, of which no sane man wants to know the full contents. She also comes bearing information. Jack Bullock is a corporate raider responsible for the death of her husband. Jack Dalton shot the man in cold blood.

Walking on the street in front of the hotel, Quinn is told the truth. She killed Jed. She had the angle. Besides, TV heroes today are too wimpy to kill anyone.

Later at the casino/stock exchange (an inspired idea), Priscilla must have someone in the poker game to hold her seat at the exchange. Stock trading is done with chips. Her trader, Cliff, is late, and she's sweating blood. To the rescue rides the Crying Man. OK, he's not on a horse but he is the cavalry. We remember from previous shows that Rembrandt knows his way around a deck of cards. But there's a catch this time. He's expected to fold every hand until Cliff arrives. This creates a humorous situation in which Rembrandt must lose to an inferior player.

When the others discover Cliff's hanged body, they don't believe it's suicide. Rembrandt is told. Now the Crying Man plays as God intended. Wade goes to the sheriff and does what she has done on other worlds: try to shame an authority figure to act responsibly. She throws Cliff's murder in his whiskered face.

Quinn faces a tougher sell with the boy, Jamie. Earlier Quinn took his stand for Priscilla and bluffed his way out of the Drexel-Bullock office. A false reputation as a deadly assassin can be as good as the real thing in the game of Make The First Move. Billy Ray is fired for his earlier support of Quinn.

Jamie's made up his mind that Quinn is the fastest gun 'Frisco's ever seen. Wade's been unable to dissuade the boy of his belief that Quinn is a gunfighter. So when Quinn finally levels with the kid, the reaction is predictable. Quinn goes from being the boy's hero to a no-good traitor. Jamie takes matters into his own hands by sneaking Quinn's gun out of the holster and running off to face the bad guys alone.

When Quinn realizes his gun is missing, he goes after Jamie. Priscilla and he head for the Drexel-Bullock building, where the corporate take-over artists are having a conference with their new hired gun, Billy the Kid! (In the script, he was Billy the Kid Gates. Wish they'd left that in.)

Jamie enters the den of monetary malefactors and gets the drop on everyone. Quinn comes in from behind but wisely doesn't try to sneak up and disarm the boy. Instead, he talks to Jamie and tells him there will be justice. Jamie has good reason not to believe the spiel but Q-ball is persuasive. Jamie allows him to take the gun.

Sometimes a TV program's gotta do what a TV program's gotta do; in this case it's a showdown over whether Priscilla keeps her company or the bad guys get it. Quinn drops his gun belt, rightly predicting that Billy the Kid won't shoot an unarmed man. Unlike Dalton, the Kid actually follows a personal code. The ploy works and Quinn demonstrates to Jamie another way to be a hero. Quinn has once again thought his way out of a life-and-death problem. He wouldn't have a chance drawing against Billy the Kid.

Quinn is so effective that Gandhi could take notes. He even wins over the crowd of frontier types, not a naturally receptive audience for a wussie. In the tradition of uncounted numbers of Hollywood westerns, the sheriff finds the courage to arrest the powerful villain despite the fact that the powerful villain will certainly ruin the brave lawman's career.

It could happen.

Right before the slide, Jamie tells his mother he thinks the Sliders are angels. But when Quinn slides last, the boy is so sorry to see him go that he calls out:

"Quinn...Quinn...come back. Come back, Quinn! Come back!"

It's better than Shane.

EL SID

Written by Jon Povill
Directed by Paris Barclay
Music by Stephen Graziano

GUEST STARS:

Jeffery Dean Morgan as Sid
Rebecca Chambers as Michele
Claude Brooks as L.J.
Jed Dixon as Leo

WITH:

Raimund Stamm as Big Jake
Reese McBeth as Blade
Sandra P. Grant as M.S.W.
Maria Herrera as Delores
Chappelle Jaffe as Gladys
Scott Swanson as Hostage

The idea of whole cities turned into prisons has been around in science fiction for a long time, besides providing the basis for much of our zoning regulations. This was a natural for Sliders because alternate history is one way of creating a prison-city. Jon Povill had already written the excellent season finale, "Luck of the Draw," so with him at the helm, story-wise, there was every reason to expect a good episode.

Well, you can't win 'em all. This was the first episode that irritated me so consistently that I could never warm up to any of it. I'm not saying that "El Sid" is the bottom of the barrel. Such honors are reserved for a number of third-season outings. But "El Sid" is handicapped by flabby logic.

The best way to prove this is to dive into the summary. The teaser reveals a world in which street violence is the social norm. (Gee, why didn't they think they were home?) The Sliders are about to escape from Turf World when Quinn ignores Arturo's sound advice not to become involved with the locals. Quinn's chivalrous nature won't let him stand by and watch a woman beaten, especially when the woman, Michelle, is having the cookies kicked out of her by the meanest S.O.B. they've encountered here, El Sid.

Quinn steps in gallantly. Sid lays him out, less gallantly, but Quinn is tough and doesn't stay down. At this point, Rembrandt performs the most intelligent action of anyone in the whole show.

He comes up from behind Sid and smashes his head with a two-by-four. The scumbag goes down.

Then the trouble begins. Michelle asks to come with Quinn because, she lies, Sid will probably kill her later. Despite previous stories in which Quinn seems to know something about human nature, he fails to pass this basic intelligence test. He believes the tramp.

Right on cue, Sid regains consciousness from a blow that should have left him unconscious for a very long time, if not dead. The gateway opens. Quinn throws Michelle into the vortex. The others follow. Bringing up the rear, it's guess who.

They reach a San Francisco that seems an environmentalist's perfect city. The air is clean and all vehicles are electric carts. As chance would have it, L.J., one of Sid's men from the other world, has a double ready and willing to cut a deal with the first Sid he sees. L.J. notices the peculiar manner of their arrival and files it away for future reference.

L.J. introduces himself and offers to get them through the system. First step, he gives them identity bracelets to wear. Next, he loads them onto his "golf cart" and drives them to a really nice hotel that happens to be "government accommodations." Surrounded by luxury, Sid and Michelle are on good terms again. Surprise, surprise.

Before the Sliders can put on their thinking caps and figure out what kind of nutty society they've landed in this time, Sid decides to prove that he's the alpha male by pushing Quinn up against a wall and threatening his life.

When Rembrandt and Arturo make a move to help, Sid threatens to snap Quinn's windpipe. Arturo calmly points out that if Sid kills Quinn he will have removed the only man who can ever get him home. Sid lets Quinn go.

Then he steps away from Quinn. Did I mention that he steps away? He doesn't have a gun. He doesn't have a knife.

This scene drives me absolutely crazy. A few minutes ago, Rembrandt took out Sid all by himself. There are four of them in the room. There is furniture that could be used as weapons. A Girl Scout has a chance against a bruiser if she notices all the objects that can be used as weapons in any furnished room.

Even though we find out later that Michelle is armed, there's no reason to assume she'd come to Sid's aid if all four jumped him. Odds are she'd stay out of it, waiting to give her allegiance to the winner, as usual.

Arturo is a big man. Quinn has an athlete's build. Rembrandt is one tough mother. And dear sweet Wade has courage flowing out every pore, as has been demonstrated time and time again. Sid is threatening to kill Quinn. The others adore Quinn. Wade would crawl over broken glass for him. Threatening to kill Quinn is also threatening to close off any hope of reaching home. The heroes do absolutely nothing to the S.O.B.

We soon learn what kind of world this is. San Francisco has been experiencing such violent earthquakes that the original population has been evacuated and the city turned into San Francisco National Penitentiary. A sentence to SFNP is an eventual death sentence because the big quake is expected to sink the entire peninsula Real Soon Now.

The authorities clearly had two choices: 1) seal off the area and leave it completely ungoverned; or 2) utilize suicidal guards, call them custodians, and have them run a system in which pairs of prisoners are linked with "buddy bracelets," so that if one commits a transgression both are summarily shot.

The choice seems obvious. Number two! That way Quinn is sure to be linked up with ... El Sid. That'll teach Quinn to let scuzballs go unpunished.

About three seconds after the identity bracelets are activated into buddy bracelets, Sid robs an ATM. This time he has his gun out. Three seconds after that, all the cops in San Francisco converge on

Sid. Meanwhile, Quinn's bracelet lights up like a Christmas tree and he realizes that his "buddy" is up to no good.

Helpful L.J. comes back into the picture and drags everyone into further peril. L.J. steals the timer. After all, he knows what it can do. He gives it to a con named Big Jake. Big Jake doesn't have it long. The guards come in and grab it from him. They have a new partner. Why, it's Sid. Pretty surprising, huh?

Leo, a top guard, and Sid plan to make the Sliders give them the secrets of their technology. They'll use torture, whether they have to or not. Then the bad guys can slide to freedom, leaving the others at the mercy of the impending earthquake.

The story concludes with the arrival of the wormhole. Rembrandt, Wade. and Arturo dive in; Quinn tries to convince Michelle to come with him; Sid attacks Quinn; and Michelle shoots Sid and slides with Quinn. There's a big earthquake. Right on time, like a train.

OK, I'll admit one really good thing about this episode. There's a sign that reads: WE APPRECIATE THAT YOU CHOOSE NOT TO STAND IN ONE PLACE FOR LONG PERIODS.

TIME AGAIN AND WORLD

Written by Jacob Epstein
Directed by Vern Gillum
Music by Anthony Marinelli

GUEST STARS:

Rebecca Gayheart as Natalie
Garry Chalk as Lt. Graves
Gary Jones as Michael Hurley
George Delhoyo as Judge John Nassau

WITH:

Garvin Cross as Alverez
Ravinder Toor as L. C.
Barry Greene as Deitrich
Lesley Ewen as O'Neill
Jed Rees as Hipster
William Sasso as Gomez Calhoun
Tom Heaton as Rummy
Robert Metcalfe as Bartender
Alfred E. Humphreys as Family Man
Brad Loree as Driver #1
Travis MacDonald as Lowlife

Back to clever writing. This time around we're afforded a glimpse of an absurdist Amerika (the Kafkaesque spelling seems appropriate). Consider a version of the US in which J. Edgar Hoover's cross-dressing inspired male cops to wear skirts; the late Hoover established a dictatorship and now his tomb is a tourist attraction to rival Lenin's; the legal drinking age has been raised to 27; President Kennedy was assassinated by circus clowns named Julius and Ethel Rosenberg (atomic spies of the 1950s in our world); and get this, the most popular TV show is *Dragnet: the Next Generation*.

Here's an attempt to make sense of "Time Again and World."

In the opening scene, Arturo quotes, "In vino veritas" (In wine there is truth). Perhaps this foreshadows the title for "In Dino, Veritas."

In a world where women's beards are in the wrong place, the Sliders witness a shooting. Wade tries to help but all the dying man can do is whisper, "Elsie—the rock, 540." He passes her a large plastic disk.

The Sliders slide to what seems to be the same world except that women are normal again. The same crime is repeated but this time Wade shouts a warning and the former victim shoots the former shooter! When Wade checks out the new victim, a cop this time, she's told the same words: "Elsie . . . the rock . . . 540." He adds a time: "8 o'clock."

After they are questioned by the authorities, our heroes enjoy a truly rare experience. They are released.

Continuing to build their inter-dimensional credit, they check in at the good old Dominion Hotel. Their stay is not as peaceful as usual because they are apprehended by a couple who warn them not to talk to the police anymore.

The threat sends Quinn and Wade right back to the constabulary.

The authorities interpret Wade's information as a meeting place and time to capture Judge Nassau, the man from the shooting.

Who is Judge Nassau? A character who plays an important role in this world's alternate history. He was one of the last defenders of constitutional rights, part of a shrinking band of strict constructionists known as the Fundamentalist Constitutionalists. The Hoover dictatorship did not countenance legalistic impediments such as the Bill of Rights—and even went beyond Lincoln's suspension of habeus corpus, giving some idea of the level of tyranny the one-time FBI director intended to impose. Rembrandt plumbs the depths of Hooverism's evil when he discovers that the dictatorship suppressed the last thirty years of rock 'n' roll.

Judge Nassau was one of the men who fought Hoover when the director seized the presidency in the early sixties, declaring martial law and altering the Constitution. The Fundamentalist Constitutionalists are now divided because they've unwittingly set up a good guy. When Wade and Quinn examine the disk that the judge in the previous world passed to Wade, it's a CD-ROM of the complete U.S. Constitution. The Hooverites are draconian. Possession of the real Constitution is a crime punishable by death.

Caught in a political whirlpool yet again, the Sliders elect to swim instead of sink. They take to undercover work like they were, uh, FBI agents. They locate the station where Radio Free America broadcasts are made.

An intense, unshaven DJ is the remaining voice for liberty in the nation. He makes it possible to fulfill the last wish of Judge Nassau—namely, to read the unabridged Constitution over the airwaves. (If only a John Galt stunt could overcome a lifetime of daily government brainwashing.)

The DJ is prepared to launch the revolution but before the blessings of liberty are again restored across the fruited plain, the Amerikan Gestapo raids the underground HQ. Quinn, Wade, and Natalie barely get away with their lives . . . and the disk.

The most promising method for saving Nassau's life is to swap the disk for his life. Reluctantly, they act on this plan, aware that Nassau might prefer death to defeat.

The exchange is made. The Hooverites betray their ideals by actually keeping their word and setting the judge free. The Sliders leave for a new world where, hopefully, the most popular album is not *Kurt Cobain: the Christmas Album*.

After they leave, we find out that Wade copied the original U.S. Constitution to the hard drive of the computer she used to decode the CD-ROM. The rebel leader Wade of the pilot episode would be proud of our girl. She starts as many revolutions as Quinn.

IN DINO VERITAS

Written by Steve Brown
Directed by Oscar L. Costo
Music by Anthony Marinelli

GUEST STARS:
Alessandra Petlin as the Ranger
Jack Kehler as the Poacher

WITH:
Brent Sheppard as Wayne Davies
Marcy Mellish as Angelica

A long with having the wittiest title of any episode, this episode provides the only occasion in science fiction to combine dinosaurs and truth devices.

The teaser of "In Dino Veritas" starts off in the world of Truth in the First Degree. Everyone is required to wear truth collars. The devices administer an electrical shock calibrated to the degree of the lie. The bigger the lie, the bigger the shock. Pathological liars would not survive. One wonders how a political system could exist at all.

At a prearranged location, Arturo and Quinn wait for the return of Wade and Rembrandt. The Crying Man is the smiling man as he is driven to the rendezvous by a new girlfriend. She is flattered and amused as he tells her little white lies about how much she means to him, but warns him to stop before the electrical jolts become serious enough to endanger his health.

Wade joins her friends without the special screwdriver they need to remove the collars. She isn't happy about failing to bring the tool. She is less happy about the man accompanying her, a reporter from *Hard Copy*.

Since serious lying is so uncommon here, people are likely to accept claims about the existence of sliding without proof. This does raise an interesting point: the collars wouldn't pose a problem for crackpots who believe their own delusions.

Left with the mystery of how historians and religious leaders avoid electrocution, the Sliders do their thing, filmed by this world's *Hard Copy*... only to enter the next world with a plop, a scrunch, and a crack. They've landed in a nest of giant eggs. Wade is the unlucky party who accidentally destroys one of the eggs.

Right away they realize they're in trouble: 1) They're in a primeval forest; 2) there's nothing remotely like San Francisco anywhere to be seen; and 3.) a very large creature with very large teeth is headed toward them, and it's roaring.

The computer-generated effects are great. The allosaurus is graceful and powerful... and fast. As small critters had to do in Long Ago Days, the Sliders live up to their name. Trees are good for climbing when something big is after you. But the humans can't stay where they are forever. The only choice is to head for higher ground.

Arturo falls and badly hurts his ankle. The others are in such a rush to get him moving again that they fail to notice he's dropped the timer/gizmo. Not until they are safely on higher ground (that the giant carnivore would have difficulty traversing) do they appreciate the full magnitude of their peril. Quinn insists that he go after the timer alone while the others seek shelter in a nearby cave. Arturo is feeling guilty and useless—the combination of losing the device and then becoming a burden on the others. His friends won't let him get away with it, and the truth collar zaps him if he tries to overdo the noble-suffering routine. Arturo finds it all quite vexing.

Not being eaten allows time for philosophical speculations. There are only two logical explanations for the presence of the allosaurus. The first is that she has been genetically "brought back" through advanced bio-technology. The second is that they've entered a world where the dinosaurs never died out—in which case there shouldn't be any humans around.

Setting themselves up as a modern stone-age family is not something we ever expected from the Sliders. Steve Brown's script takes full advantage of the truth collars to keep the basic survival story moving in unexpected directions.

The key is Arturo. His virtues keep getting him punished. When asked if he can make it to the cave with his busted ankle, he is promptly zapped for trying to be a real trouper. Inside the cave, Arturo is punished by the collar when he attempts to put Wade and Rembrandt at ease.

There are sufficient elements here for a whole episode, but *Sliders* likes to throw in unexpected curves. When the allosaurus finds them (there must be another way to the cave) and peers in at them from a hole in the roof, Wade throws a rock at its eye. So a dinosaur ranger appears and tells her to stop tormenting the beast.

Dinosaur ranger?

This very uptight woman (acting kudos for Alessandra Petlin) challenges Wade with: "Are you trying to blind her? You already killed her baby." The ranger fills them in on the basics. They are trespassing in the San Francisco National Dinosaur Preserve and Spotted Owl Sanctuary.

Unfortunately, as a professional science-fiction writer, it's my job to nitpick. How is it possible for dinosaurs and humans to co-exist in the natural order of things? The same planetary changes that removed the dinosaurs from center stage placed mammals at center stage, an evolutionary precondition for human beings' becoming masters of the world. Wade even refers to the current theory of a comet's colliding with the Earth, the event that started the evolutionary ball rolling in our favor.

The ranger is a hologram. No matter what our heroes say or do, the ranger is convinced they are poachers who have been in the preserve for weeks. A huge black market exists for dinosaur organs and tissue for medical purposes, as well as folk remedies.

Wade appeals to the ranger for help in locating Quinn. The ranger coldly mentions having seen human remains that might be their missing companion. When Wade makes an attempt at proving the truth collars are genuine, as a means of proving her truthfulness, all she succeeds in doing is hurting herself. The ranger assumes it's all an act. Got to watch out for those actors.

The ranger informs them that she has dispatched an arrest team. The good news is that it will take some time for the arrest team to arrive. Rembrandt volunteers to go look for Quinn. When the ranger tells him not to go, he reminds her that she's only a hologram and tells her to go to hell. Although Rembrandt fails to find Quinn, the hungry dinosaur finds him and it looks bad until... he's rescued by the real poacher. The two return to the cave, where the poacher demonstrates a neat trick. He has a device that jams the ranger's holographic signal.

The human remains the ranger sighted were this man's buddy. Raptors got him. After days in the bush—dirty, exhausted, and partnerless—he is not in a good mood. He's convinced that if the newcomers hadn't complicated matters he would have avoided detection. They can make it up to him by helping transport his goods out of the park before the arrest team arrives.

Complicating matters is the state of Arturo's health. His foot is swollen and he's running a fever. Wade's convinced that the ankle's broken. In addition, none of them want to give up on Quinn. So they politely decline the poacher's offer to throw in with him. He shows them how to do a proper splint for Arturo's injury. Then he backs up his insistence with an elephant gun.

More exhausted than his prisoners, the poacher falls asleep first. Light on her feet, and with light fingers to match, Wade lifts the man's jamming device and tries to reestablish contact with the ranger—with no immediate success. Then she sneaks outside to look for Quinn herself.

Once again, the allosaurus does a better job of finding humans than vice versa. A flesh-eating dinosaur is about to devour Wade. Yum. But wait, who is that rushing to the rescue? Why, it's Quinn.

But wait, who is that also rushing to the rescue? Why, it's the poacher—and a good thing, too. Quinn is shouting and trying to distract the monster but his only weapon is a rock. The poacher has his elephant gun and engages Mama Dinosaur's attention long enough for Quinn to get Wade away. Unfortunately for the poacher, his elephant gun jams and he might as well have a rock to throw at nature's most efficient land-based eating machine. Quinn and Wade hear the man's scream. The big cheat is that we don't get to see him gobbled up.

Back at the cave, Quinn tells of his adventures playing hide-and-seek with the allosaurus in his fruitless search for the timer. He was penned up for a long stretch in a low outcropping of rock and there was no way to communicate. Together again, the Sliders:

1.) unjam the signal and reestablish contact with the ranger, who has a change of heart—one glance at Quinn works wonders—and informs them she has found the location of the timer at the bottom of the hill;

2) finally remove those damned truth collars using equipment of the late poacher;

3) go through the poacher's supplies and find vials of dinosaur at-
   tractents and repellents, unlabeled and stinking to high heaven;
   and

4) guess right on the repellents, make it down the hill to the timer
   with seconds to spare, and slide to ...

An archeological dig where they happen to damage a valuable
fossil. One guess as to what kind of fossil!

POST-TRAUMATIC SLIDE SYNDROME

Written by Nan Hagen
Directed by Adam Nimoy
Music by Stephen Graziano

GUEST STARS:
Kristoffer Tabori as Dr. Whelan
Stacy Grant as Miss Vonbaeck

WITH:
Don MacKay as Artie Field
Deanne Henry as Mrs. Mallory
Carlton Watson as Sebastian Smith
Tom Picket as Leroy Hopkins
Brian Arnold as Barry King
Linda Ko as Tanika
Tina Klassen as Miss Jennings
Mike Mitchell as Guard

The first title of this script was "Our So-Called Lives." A good thing it was changed to one of the best titles. Rembrandt gets off one of the most quotable phrases ever, and here it is: "Condemned to wander the interdimensional vortex like nomads." Now that's writin'!

Imagine a world where someone would try to steal the credit for discovering how to slide between dimensions. Every week tuning into *Sliders*, I wondered how the world at large might respond to the announcement that someone had traveled between dimensions. How many would even care? Even though "Post-Traumatic Slide Syndrome" is about a dishonest character who makes this announcement, the public response is all that could be desired: a positive reaction to the vision of a new adventure for mankind.

The story begins with Rembrandt in a psychiatrist's office telling the doctor all about sliding. The doctor takes notes and asks his patient to continue and please tell him what precipitated his personal crisis. The main story begins with the four's arrival in a familiar looking San Francisco, this time arguing over the best order in which to slide.

First stop is Quinn's house. He wants to believe that he's found his mother. She's thrilled to hear about the exploits of her son. Wade phones home, reaching what seems to be her family on the other end, and they've been missing her for the correct period of time. She can't wait to see them.

Rembrandt is shown what he assumes is the original basement for the first time, reminding him of the day his red Cadillac was sucked into the vortex. Everything seems to be checking out.

The professor makes a crucial suggestion: that if they have returned home, they agree to keep the nature of sliding a secret until they learn how to control the process. Rembrandt is disgruntled about putting off the incredible publicity he will receive. Despite reservations, they agree to Arturo's plan.

The next day Arturo goes to his old campus, where he strikes up a peculiar conversation with his teaching assistant. He tells her he's glad to be back. She doesn't behave as though he's been away.

The Crying Man contacts his agent. He's the same one we saw in the pilot—Artie. Unable to tell the man where he's really been, he concocts a cock-and-bull story about playing Outer Mongolia. It's tough to be an agent. Rembrandt gets nowhere fast so in desperation he tells Artie the real story with the understanding that they will keep it under wraps until the Sliders go public.

Then something really weird happens. Arturo goes on television and announces the existence of sliding and takes sole credit for it. For proof, Arturo holds up a small arrowhead and says it's crafted from a space-age titanium alloy from a world where Europe never colonized the Americas.

Later Rembrandt and Wade meet with Quinn, both insisting that he can't stand by and let Arturo steal his achievement. Quinn refuses to publicly denounce Arturo. He is sticking to the original agreement, partly because he senses that something is badly out of whack.

Quinn is again disappointed when Wade and Rembrandt admit they've gone public, too—but only after the public announcement by Arturo made secrecy a moot issue. *Newsweek* is serializing Wade's diary, and the Crying Man has offers from three major recording labels.

While Wade and Rembrandt deal with the personal ramifications and commercial possibilities, Quinn thinks of the big picture and he looks for significant details. He finds one—an old newspaper headline declaring the 49ers victors over the Jets in Superbowl XIX.

The trouble is that Wade and Rembrandt are so thrilled to reconnect with their old lives that they fail to appreciate the significance of Quinn's knowledge of sports statistics. Something is wrong. From this moment on, the battle lines are drawn. Quinn tells his friends they are not home—but they believe he's denying the fact of their return as a way of emotionally dealing with Arturo's betrayal.

Quinn becomes more uneasy when a burglar breaks into his basement and steals the timer/gizmo. Meanwhile, Arturo holds a press conference at which he explains sliding with nifty models of parallel Earths. Quinn's presence doesn't alter his presentation one whit. If anything, he becomes more belligerent and tells Quinn to be realistic. He argues that they will probably never find a world closer to home than this one and that the time has come to make the best of it.

But Quinn's instincts tell him something is more wrong than only what's on the surface. Arturo always had a big ego but never like this, downplaying Quinn's work and unveiling a huge statue of himself as the Father of Sliding.

Wade is having a tough enough time digesting the dimensions of Arturo's betrayal without Quinn's continually badgering her that her loving family is really someone else's loving family. He keeps hitting her with discrepancies, such as a missing asterisk from Roger Marris' home-run record on a famous baseball card. She denies the mounting evidence until one shocking moment that destroys all her faith in this world and throws her back again to the only certainty in her life: a lanky, quirky, one-of-a-kind genius who cares about her very much.

It is possible to stay in San Francisco for days and not notice the Golden Gate Bridge. Especially when it's not the Golden Gate Bridge. Wade stares at the familiar landmark and its color: blue as the water it spans, blue as Quinn's eyes. In this world it's called the Azure Gate Bridge.

Rembrandt's rude awakening comes courtesy of his rude backup singers, the Topps, who share writing credit on his songs in this world. Besides which, they are making insane demands they never made back home. They want to cry along with him on the stage. Some things simply aren't done. Some lines are not crossed. And sometimes a man's gotta slide when a man's gotta slide.

They haven't forgotten the Arturo problem. There will be no sliding without the equipment. Wade's informed Quinn that the timer is on display at the Museum of Science. They go for it and trigger the security alarms. They are caught—red faced and red handed. The timer/gizmo on display was a fake. Well, they wouldn't have slid without their companions.

About now we're reminded that Rembrandt is telling this story to a psychiatrist, who conveniently takes a break to go tell his assistant to send for a medical team to come and take Rembrandt to the booby hatch.

Rembrandt resumes the tale for the doctor's, and our, edification. He bailed Quinn and Wade out of jail and then they went to Arturo's home, deducing that he must have the real timer/gizmo there. In the basement, they find the professor shackled to a water pipe. He warns them about an insane Arturo double in this world.

Only Quinn has the right to say the "I told you so." At least he suspected something was fishy. Their Arturo was too decent a man to ever pull a stunt like that. And he'd gone through far too much with them to do such a thing.

In this world, Professor Arturo did not slide with the others. He lost his nerve. Ever since, he's been biding his time, planning to take credit for sliding if the opportunity ever presented itself. Freed from his bonds, Arturo opens a drawer where he says he saw his double put the timer.

Down the stairs comes Arturo, timer in hand, insisting he's the real Arturo and that he'd gotten away from his double, had tied him up, and had been looking for the others. Although it wouldn't make any difference for deciding who is who, they are dressed the same. When they fight, we lose track of who was chained up and who was on the stairs.

One Arturo knocks out the other, and Rembrandt says to the one who runs with them that he'd better be the right one. They return to Quinn's house and prepare for the slide when who should join them but the other Arturo. Quinn suggests they take both with them and sort it out in the next world, but the two Arturo's fight again, and one slides. One is left behind to say, "Oh, my God."

The epilogue occurs back at the shrink's office. It's totally predictable and totally fun. Rembrandt's lost track of the time so the others come find him. Barging past the assistant, they enter the doctor's sanctum, open the gateway, and slide out of there. Rembrandt thanks the doc and slides last, the polite thing to do.

The last shot is of the psychiatrist being carried out on a stretcher, describing the pretty tunnel in the air. No doubt his colleagues will prescribe a visit from the Amazing Randi, who will explain how any stage magician could fake the wormhole.

OBSESSION

Teleplay by Jon Povill
Story by Jon Povill and Steve Brown
Directed by Paris Barclay
Music by Stephen Graziano

GUEST CAST:
James Patrick Stuart as Derek Bond
Heather Hanson as Dominique
Isaac Hayes as the Prime Oracle

WITH:
Malcolm Stewart as Regent
Sandra P. Grant as Melanie
Paul McGillion as First Officer
Hiro Kanagawa as Henry
Gillian Carfra as Young Woman

What a relief to have another good script by Jon Povill. Takes the curse off "El Sid." Credit must also go to Steve Brown for collaborating on the story. Some fans have called this the woman's romance installment, and maybe it is; but there's nothing wrong with that.

Science fiction has always had an uneasy alliance with matters of the heart, so much is sci-fi a product of the intellect. Even so, many important science-fiction writers have brought mature sexual relationships into their work, and even gone on to the more difficult and controversial portrayal of adolescent relationships.

Besides tackling a strong emotional subject, "Obsession" treats the idea of psychic powers intelligently, and develops an alternate history in which such powers become a concern of the State. The episode begins with a lushly romantic teaser, complete with soft lighting and fancy costumes. A handsome young man, garbed in aristocratic finery, rides an equally handsome horse whilst (seems the right place to say "whilst") fair Wade, attired as a maid, long hair flying, sits astride another proud steed.

The young lovers have a slight problem. This is no mere dalliance, no sowing of a young lord's wild oats. He intends to marry the lass. No fool she, Wade is doubtful that the young man's father will approve the match. After all, in olden days there were class barriers that no longer exist, except for all the cases in which they do.

Wade wakes up from a dream. It's nearly time for the slide. Our hardy band exits the Dominion Hotel onto a street that looks like Calcutta, complete with an unattended cow. San Francisco is that kind of town. They slide to a world where . . .

Wade's dream takes on a life of its own. The man from her dream is waiting for them. He climbs off a motorcycle and presents her with a bouquet of roses. He's been waiting for her and addresses her by name.

His name is Derek Bond. He's a seer. He knows everyone by name. After a little verbal sparring, the Sliders more or less accept the situation. To Quinn's discomfort, Wade accepts Bond's invitation to dine with him that evening. They don't have to tell him they'll be at the Dominion Hotel. (The cross-dimensional chain must maintain a high standard of service.)

The Sliders have a bad habit of running into Very Important People every time they reach a new world. Derek Bond is in line to become the Prime Oracle, the official seer to the president of the United States—effectively the most powerful man in the country. Bond is convinced that Wade and he were lovers in a past life. So there's some reincarnation thrown in for good measure.

The oracles are extremely important to this society. For example, they diagnose patients (there are no X-rays). They also head crimes off at the pass. They hold life-and-death powers beyond that of any politician.

James Patrick Stuart plays Derek Bond as arrogant but balanced on the ethical edge so that we're never sure if he'll turn out to be a good guy or a bad guy. Sabrina Lloyd matches his performance with ambivalence of her own. She is vulnerable but unwilling to surrender her identity to anyone, even the man of her dreams.

Isaac Hayes has a cameo as the Prime Oracle who must decide between Derek and a woman named Melanie for his replacement. As all three have psychic powers, the scene is lots of fun. No pulling the wool over anyone's eyes. The Prime Oracle tells Melanie that she has more power than Derek. He tells Derek that he has more discipline. He considers the latter more important.

Derek is his own worst enemy. He pushes too hard and makes a crucial error when he invites Wade into a room reconstructed from her childhood memories. There's no way he could have know about the room without rooting around in her mind without permission. Wade is ticked off. He violated her rights by trespassing on her most personal memories.

She finally decides to turn down Derek's offer. His mind is disciplined, he has vast mental powers, and he has one more thing: impatience with anyone who defies him. This is a perfect combination for a dictator. He places Wade under house arrest.

Her first escape attempt—a plan that would work in most other situations—is easily thwarted by an opponent who can read her mind. Wade is completely trapped. None of her usual ploys will get her out of this one. What to do? Quinn is going out of his mind. Not even the president of the United States dares interfere with someone about to become Prime Oracle.

Arturo and Rembrandt realize they are Wade's only hope because Quinn is too emotionally involved. The Crying Man provides the key to their plan with a doctor he's gotten to know who doesn't believe the powerful have the right to trample on others.

The result: Wade seems to commit suicide. Heavily drugged and slurring her speech, she telephones Quinn to say goodbye. Nearly hysterical, Quinn rushes to her side. He confronts Derek for having caused the death of a woman they both adore. Quinn's emotions come out in such a torrent that Derek can't pick up any other mental energy in Wade's bedroom.

The crucial element of the plan was that even a powerful seer would be unable to read the deep, slumbering mind of his beloved if Quinn happened to be in the room. So, dejected and crushed, Derek Bond allows Quinn to remove the "body."

Quinn accompanies Wade in an ambulance to a prearranged rendezvous with Arturo and Rembrandt. There they tell him what they couldn't risk letting him know beforehand. The doctor revives Wade. With only a few minutes before the slide, it seems nothing else can go wrong.

The moment Wade regains consciousness, Derek detects her mind—even at such a distance (the man is good). Accompanied by his minions, he rushes to her side . . . and reaches her before the slide. Surprisingly, he no longer intends to impede them. Wade was his destiny, all right, in bringing about a sea change in his soul. The Prime Oracle probably knew more than he let on.

The ultimate test for Derek is to allow the great love of his life to leave him. He is left with power, fame, authority, wealth . . . and an empty heart.

GREATFELLAS

Teleplay by Scott Smith Miller
Story by Sean Clark and Scott Smith Miller
Directed by Allan Eastman
Music by Stephen Graziano

GUEST CAST:

Donnelly Rhodes as Ben Greenfeld
Sarah Strange as Leah Greenfield
Benjamin Ratner as Tommy Greenfeld
Venus Terzo as June

SPECIAL APPEARANCE BY:

Mel Tormé as Himself

WITH:

Clinton Derricks-Carroll as Rembrandt 2
Byron Lucas as John
William Sasso as Gomez Calhoun
Jano Frandsen as Joseph Biacchi
Ted Cole as Agent Reid
Joe Maffei as Dabelle Patriarch
Russell Ferrier as Bartender
Aurelio Di Nunzio as Pit Boss
Doug Cameron as Maitre D'

"Greatfellas" counts as a very personal episode of *Sliders* because Tracy Tormé asked his father to play himself with one alternate history twist: Mel Tormé is a country and western singer!

Being in a world where 84 percent of the population attended law school would put anyone in the mood for a world run by gangsters. The Sliders are at a hamburger stand. Rembrandt, Wade, and Quinn are sitting at one of the outdoor tables. Arturo turns away from the service window, frustrated that he doesn't have any food. He informs his comrades that ordering food here is more complicated than buying a house.

Rembrandt remains unconvinced. Fear that the next world may turn out to be a vegetarian nightmare means that he wants a greasy, juicy hamburger now. He orders a Super Carnivore burger, fries, and coke for himself. For Arturo and Quinn he orders two Whammy burgers. That's as far as he gets.

The waiter behind the counter requires: 1) salmonella insurance; 2) carbonated release forms; 3) a picture I.D.; and 4) a doctor's note verifying a cholesterol count under two hundred. This, my friends, is why we need a show like *Sliders*. It has what *Star Trek* will never have—a bad attitude.

In the few minutes remaining before the slide, Rembrandt bumps into a woman and makes the mistake of apologizing in front of witnesses, an admission of guilt. Faster than you can say medical damages, a lawyer offers to take the case. The gateway opens not a moment too soon, but not before Rembrandt generously agrees to let the apoplectic ambulance chaser take the case with the understanding he can bill Rembrandt on another Earth.

Our heroes have slid into territories more dangerous than a wedding, but not often. Especially when powerful gangster families, one Italian and one Jewish, are nervously tying the knot. Rembrandt makes a spectacular entrance and ends up wearing some of the floral arrangements. Everyone at the wedding pulls out handguns in unison and trains them on Rembrandt. The good news is that no one pulls the trigger.

As has happened before, one of the Sliders is mistaken for himself. The Rembrandt of this world must be fairly important.

He is treated with such healthy respect that, once the initial shock is over, everyone reholsters their pieces. Then Rembrandt notices the old crooner himself, Mel Tormé, and goes over to say hello—a great bit. (See the interview with Cleavant Derricks.)

Then Rembrandt calls it a day and wishes for everyone to continue with the wedding. The other Sliders stand in the background and wait for the Crying Man to extricate himself from this one.

In short order, the Sliders receive their crash course in current events. Rembrandt Brown in this world is in charge of the Incorruptibles. He must be having flashbacks to J. Edgar Hoover World. Here, Rembrandt is the FBI director. The wedding they gate-crashed is a major political event, a merger of the Greenfelds, who control California, and the DaBellos, who control Nevada. The alternate history that makes this possible is that Prohibition was never repealed.

The Incorruptibles have some clout, though. Rembrandt and his party are given a good room at . . . guess which hotel! Quinn receives a visit from an angry Mel Tormé. In this world, he's not only a famous singer but also an FBI informant. He complains that Rembrandt fingered him at the wedding. Here he'd worked hard to be accepted by the Greenfelds and now they suspect him. Tormé tells Quinn to pass a simple message to Rembrandt—that he should wait until Mel gives the signal before he gives anything to reporters. Before cutting out, he tells Quinn he'll be doing a double set at the Doubloon.

Next up at bat is one of the Greenfelds, who gives Rembrandt a $100,000 bribe. At the time, it seems as if the most prudent course of action is to take it, but Quinn doesn't like the idea of tarnishing the image of FBI director Brown. As usual, Arturo speaks for the practical side. All they need do is lay low for twenty-seven hours and then slide. But...

Quinn, money in hand, attends the Mel Tormé concert with the idea he may be able to return the cash. Fans of the crooner enjoy the best gag of the show when they see a Nashville version of Tormé.

Seems that every time Arturo's good advice is ignored, trouble follows shortly thereafter. Quinn is robbed when he involves himself in a situation that has the look of a set-up. Come on, Quinn! Start picking up on this stuff, man.

Her name is June. She robs him blind.

Despite this new setback, Mel agrees to help Quinn but is apparently blown up by a car bomb when he turns on the ignition. Quinn is devastated. Jerry O'Connell has the same expression a loving son would have if he lost his father before his eyes. The moment touches the heart.

When FBI director Rembrandt Brown blows into town, he has his work cut out for him. Despite all the confusion and chaos the Sliders have left in their wake, Quinn and Wade's obsession for justice will make up for a lot.

Support for the good guys comes from the bride-to-be. She goes to the Sliders' hotel room, convinced they are the authentic Incorruptibles. She brings a financial ledger that can nail everyone. Naturally, she wants protective custody and is displeased when Rembrandt informs her that he is not the real McCoy.

Leaving the bride-not-to-be in the room, Wade and Arturo go to the local FBI office, a pathetic fly-by-night operation in an old rundown building. Turns out the witness protection program ran out of money years ago. What's more, the director seems disturbingly unhelpful for a man with his kind of reputation.

Desperate to get the information into friendly hands, Arturo and Wade turn to District Attorney Joey Biacchi, whose TV ads proclaim: Joe Biacchi for Governor—because Ronald Reagan is just too soft on crime. In this world, Reagan is running for governor again after being president.

Biacchi invites them into his limo, and everyone watching television knows instantly that he's a crook who is going to set them up. Only our heroes fail to notice the obvious clues. They should have turned to Reagan for help.

While this is going on, one of the neatest scenes of the series takes place at the casino. Quinn confronts June about ripping him off. She tells him that she no longer has the money. Not even the threat of turning her over to the Greenfelds makes her panic, but she does cough up five thousand, which she says is all that remains after gambling the rest away.

Demonstrating that he'll never make it as a pimp, Quinn settles for the five G's (and nothing more). Now he can use his amazing brain to recover all the missing loot. He goes to the blackjack table, where he wins back the full amount by "counting cards," keeping track of five decks in play. Quinn's line: "Blackjack's not so dissimilar from advanced number theory."

Now that Quinn has his money back in hand, the climax can't be far behind. This one's right out of a Republic serial. The good guys are captured and tied up. The bad guys lecture them about the terrible things that will happen to them if the Greenfeld daughter is not returned. The sleaziest of the gunmen threatens to kill one of our heroes to convince the others of the gravity of the situation. Wouldn't you know it, he's gonna shoot Wade first! What's the matter with villains today?

Before the creepy gunman commits his crime against nature, the FBI arrives and there's a shootout. Miraculously, no stray bullet hits any nice person.

The Sliders reach the next world by sliding, instead of crossing that big river in the sky. Right before they depart, Quinn spots Mel Tormé in the shadows. Takes more than a car bomb to take out a golden age crooner.

THE YOUNG AND THE RELENTLESS

Teleplay by T. Edward Anthony and Von Whisenhant
Story by Michael X. Farrara, T. Edward Anthony, and Von
  Whisenhant
Directed by Richard Compton
Music by Anthony Marinelli

GUEST CAST:
  Laura Harris as Margo
  Russell Porter as Kenny Hatcher
  Kristy Cohen as Tiffany
  August Kyle Alisharan as Kyle Beck

WITH:
  Paul Jarrett as Razor Gillette
  Richard Cox as Richard Gordon
  Michael Woolvett as Judge
  Britt Lind as Joanne
  Elisabeth Rosen as Melanie White
  Trevor Roberts as Bartender
  Jason Emanuel as Policeman #1
  Paul Anderson as Kromagg

This is another good showcase for Sabrina Lloyd. The sweet girl-next-door finally has a chance to play a complete villain.

I knew she loved it even before I asked in the interview how she liked playing a cold-hearted bitch.

As for the theme of "The Young and the Relentless," this is one of the more important episodes of *Sliders* in my book (which is the one you're holding). The premise of a world where youth is exalted is another tried-and-true science fiction idea.

Watching this episode gave me a lot to think about.

Consider, for a moment, the scam that the baby boom generation is trying to pull off. (I'm a card-carrying member of the boomer generation.) We have reproduced far below previous levels and divorced at higher levels. Consumed with guilt for having some fun in the sixties and seventies, and maybe making a buck in the eighties, we want to make certain that our kids live the impeccable moral life we never wanted for ourselves. No sex. No drinking. No smoking. No violent entertainment. The worst we expect from them in return is bad music and lousy fashion sense.

With a smaller generation coming behind us (because every baby born is proof of unsafe sex!), we expect these same kids who aren't supposed to have any fun to work like slaves so we can collect Social Security. We give this conspiracy against a whole generation several names: "protecting the children," "social responsibility," "family values," and "good citizenship." If there's any justice, this will be a recipe for revolution.

With that in mind, let's visit the highly entertaining world of "The Young and the Relentless." It all began when President Howard Stern lowered the voting age to nine. A twenty-year-old is running for the highest office in the land. The Supreme Court has upheld a decision to suspend Social Security. Best of all, elderly people have a curfew. Well, if that's what it takes to curb their bad driving.

The Sliders wind up in the back yard of a large estate that just happens to belong to the alternate Quinn and Wade of this world, who are married. Or were. The Quinn of this world is recently deceased, his body having been found floating face down in his swimming pool.

Wade's alternate is initially shocked to see her husband alive again, but she doesn't allow a beat to pass before asking our Quinn to stand in for her late husband. The Quinn of this world was known as Q.R. (shades of J.R. from Dallas), and he became a big tycoon in his early twenties. Right before his death, he was on the verge of selling Edulearn, a new educational tool, to the state legislature. Wade #2 wants Quinn #1 to help push through the deal.

Edulearn is a software program that would make public schools obsolete, accelerating the educational process within the home. Teachers would no longer have a function (except maybe as a T-chip, installed to block out knowledge the kids aren't supposed to have— the real function of public schools). Quinn at first goes along with the idea because he is a techie and is computer friendly. A computer-based education system could be an improvement over the classroom, but he's not willing to take it on blind faith.

Not surprisingly, he comes across evidence that the Edulearn program is a hoax, a gigantic advertisement for Impact Cola. Quinn is ready to jump ship but he miscalculates. The kind of people ruthless enough to try something of this magnitude are ruthless enough to play rough with anyone who comes into their orbit. Gillette, one of Wade #2's guardians, steals the timer/gizmo, leaving Quinn with no alternative but to go along with Edulearn if he ever wants to slide again.

The social satire is not explored as fully as it might have been but there's only so much that can be worked into one hour of television and still leave room for the commercials. One wonderful scene shows Rembrandt and Arturo refused service in a bar because they are over thirty. Neither intends to put up with second-class citizen status while breath remains. When they defend themselves against force, they are arrested for starting a brawl.

The courtroom scene is funnier than anything on even *The People's Court*. They are assigned a seventeen-year-old public defender, female. The judge is eighteen, male, and has the hots for the defender. Instead of recognizing potential benefits from the situation, Arturo behaves in characteristic fashion. The judgment is not good, leaving the two elderly Sliders with no alternative but to escape on their way to jail.

While the professor and the Crying Man are experiencing the downside of empowered youth, Quinn and Wade see this frantic, hyper society from the inside. Quinn is confronted by a woman named Melanie who claims that Wade's alternate masterminded the murder of her husband. This inspires Quinn to examine the coroner's report, in which he finds inconsistencies. Convinced that he's dealing with actual evil, he spills his guts to our Wade, and the two of them plan to recover the timer/gizmo.

By this point in the story, the revelation of murder doesn't really come as a shock. Lloyd has played the other Wade so cold that killing someone seems a perfectly logical move for her. We are the sum total of the choices we make, the values we choose to uphold . . . or betray.

Further investigation leads to the discovery that Wade #2 is more than a one-time killer. What does our Wade feel when contemplating a version of herself who would murder the man they both supposedly love? The Quinn of this world must have had something in common with our Quinn in terms of ethical standards. He paid for it with his life.

Throughout the series, Wade is even more impulsive than Quinn when encountering situations that provoke moral outrage. The strength to act makes for heroes . . . and villains. Our Wade confronts what she could have become through a series of wrong choices and ultimately corrupted values.

"The Young and the Relentless" forces Wade and Quinn to fight fire with fire. This they do with a truly clever ruse. They realize they have a tremendous advantage they've yet to exploit. They make two videotapes. One features our Wade dressed to the nines and wearing heavier makeup so that she looks like Wade #2 (somewhere there's an alternate Earth where the good girls wear heavy makeup). Wade on the tape confesses to the murder of Melanie's husband. The second tape is even more damning, showing Wade and Quinn staging the murder of this world's Quinn. Quite a double bill, with Wade #2 as the star.

As if to offset this excellent plan, Quinn and Wade make an unforgivable error. It never occurs to them to bring a weapon when they confront Wade #2. Naturally, Wade #2 pulls a gun. A killer is not going to surrender without a fight. Villains who are willing to risk everything don't stop taking risks if there's the remotest chance of victory. The great detective in classic mysteries doesn't need a gun when he reveals that Rodney is the killer because half the metropolitan police force is situated nearby should the blighter attempt to flee. Or, to quote Sherlock Holmes, "Watson, your revolver."

In the grand tradition of loquacious villains, Wade #2 wastes precious time letting them in on her latest scheme. Our Wade provides Wade #2 with an easy way to fake suicide. A good plan. A nice throwaway line is that a good place to start over is Florida because retirement age there is extended all the way to forty.

Speech over, it looks bad for our heroes but they are saved by a plot twist, the next best thing to packing iron. Gillette enters the picture. He's had a bellyful of Wade #2. He won't go along with her anymore, especially now that he's become the new heir to Q.R.'s fortune.

When Gillette goes for his gun, Wade #2 shoots him, giving Quinn a chance to tackle her before she can shoot anyone else. The gun goes flying. In the struggle, Wade #2 is about to strike Quinn with a heavy ashtray when our Wade steps into the fray, gun in hand. The acting, directing, and editing are all top notch.

We never doubt that the good Wade is willing to pull the trigger on the bad Wade.

The villainess is carted off to jail. As fate would have it, Arturo and Rembrandt just happen to be returning from jail, where they finally wound up after their trial. To Arturo's surprise, the seventeen-year-old defender was good at her job and the charges were dismissed.

The four are reunited and ready to slide into next week. They should have stayed in Young World if only they could. An epilogue sets the stage for the most sinister episode of the series.

Gillette is aboard some kind of spaceship (!) and undergoing interrogation. The off-screen personage never speaks, but the way Gillette defensively answers unspoken questions can only mean telepathy. He apologizes for not doing a better job of keeping track of the Sliders, one in particular. We learn Gillette's double in this world was done away with to make room for this Gillette. Whoever is keeping tabs on the Sliders is a Slider.

INVASION

Written by Tracy Tormé
Directed by Richard Compton

GUEST STARS:

Lee Weaver as Hilton Brown
Una Damon as Mary
Robert Lewis as Mr. Clarke
Franciose Najda as French Waiter
Pierre Martineau as French Bread Man
Jason Gaffney as Prisoner

The scariest episode of *Sliders* would have made a fine feature film. It also boasts an original idea for a menace. There's a lot of science fiction about parallel Earths but none I've run across with anything quite like the Kromaggs. Tormé's script takes off from the idea of an Earth where primate evolution took a decidedly different path. A far more dangerous killer ape than even Homo sapiens masters its world and is able only to unite against the common enemy of Homo sapiens.

In a pattern not dissimilar to our own, the Kromaggs reach high-tech civilization prodded on by war and conquest. They also discover sliding and are more advanced than Quinn. The Kromaggs control their sliding. Imagine their disquiet when they learn that the hated Homo sapiens dominates all other dimensions. Well, at least the Kromaggs could comfort themselves about having a monopoly on sliding... until finding out about Quinn Mallory!

As the only humanoid monsters on *Sliders*, the Kromaggs benefitted from careful makeup. The scenes in which they torment humans by extracting visions from the past are strong stuff.

The story begins with one of the best gags. Arturo, Wade, and Quinn all slide as usual, but this time Rembrandt is wearing goggles and an assortment of small cushions and pillows.

It's a great bit of business. Rembrandt has proven himself to be a practical inventor.

The Sliders have entered an empty fair ground. It's always a creepy feeling to be in an environment associated with crowds after it's been abandoned. The only signs of recent activity are giant graffiti messages: THE KROMAGGS ARE COMING! THE END IS HERE!

The last thing they want to run across is a dire warning just as the timer starts to act up. Quinn pinpoints the source of the disturbance in the north. They walk in that direction to see if they can ascertain the problem.

Quinn tells Arturo that whatever is affecting the timer/gizmo must be giving off a powerful electromagnetic pulse on the same frequency as the timer. That's when they hear the sound—a deep hum combined with crackling static that puts the teeth on edge.

Turning a corner, they see a manta-ray-shaped flying ship. When the ship accelerates and heads straight for them, Quinn saves the day by using the timer. He reasons that if the timer works on the same electrical wavelength as the alien ship, he should be able to jam the ship's controls. Theory is put into practice, throwing the craft's gyros into chaos so badly that it crashes.

Instead of hoofing it out of there, they make the courageous choice to explore the crashed ship. Knowledge is power, except when it forms a noose around your neck. Arturo observes that the ship seems to be made of an organic metal. As he and Quinn discuss the possibility of its being of extraterrestrial origin, a man in a fancy suit approaches and informs them that the ship is not from outer space.

The Sliders want to know about the Kromaggs. The dude will only say they are marauders who eat human eyes. This bit of intelligence is sufficient for Rembrandt and Wade to recommend a speedy exit, but Quinn and Arturo's scientific curiosity is not so easily satisfied. Wade figures out that the strange man is an inhabitant of a local insane asylum who politely departs with two hookers. Our heroes have done enough sliding to know that they shouldn't discount a story just because a crazy person is telling it.

Inside the craft, it's like the science fair from hell. At least the atmosphere is a familiar oxygen-nitrogen mix and they have no difficulty breathing. Strange as the ship is, nothing about it is more disturbing than their discovery of the dead Kromagg pilot. The human elements of the apelike countenance are not at all attractive to human eyes. Quinn realizes that he killed the creature. Its neck broke during the crash. Arturo reminds Quinn that he has killed an invading alien soldier.

Before they can make a full study of the control console, Arturo triggers an alarm when he removes a bracelet off the dead pilot's wrist. They rejoin the others just as two Kromagg soldiers emerge from around a corner and begin firing laser weapons at them and calling out in a guttural, unknown language.

With the removal of the manta ship's interference, the timer is working again. Twenty-three seconds to slide. All they have to do is stay alive.

The vortex opens on schedule. Arturo and Rembrandt slide first. Before Quinn and Wade follow, they witness a terrifying sight: one of the manta ships emerging from a red wormhole. The Kromaggs are Sliders.

The next world returns us to more familiar alternate history country. North America took a different turn and has become New France. The San Francisco region is the city of Versailles West. John Rhys-Davies plays Arturo especially well here, extracting maximum humor from the situation.

In an outdoor cafe, Arturo and a French waiter put on a performance for the others. When Arturo is complimented for his forbearance, especially after the waiter has disparaged the cuisine of that little island called England, the good professor reminds his companions that the little battle won't be over until the waiter sees his tip.

After this pleasant interlude, Arturo reveals that he took a piece of Kromagg technology that looks like a wristwatch. Quinn doesn't think his mentor had the right to do so. The discussion is rendered academic when the timepiece begins to glow red. A red wormhole opens and a Kromagg ship enters near its quarry. The damned "watch" acts as a homing device. Before Quinn can activate the timer/gizmo to disable the Manta, all four of them are zapped with a ray that knocks them out. The Kromaggs learn from mistakes and have come prepared.

The Kromaggs retrieve the device and take the humans prisoner. Unlike other opponents who have seized Quinn's device, the Kromaggs know sliding technology when they see it, even if it's of a radically different design.

The Sliders regain consciousness on Earth 1-1-3, a barren rock where life never developed. Being informed that they are guests of the Kromagg Dynasty is their only evidence of the aliens' sense of humor. The Kromaggs fear the Sliders are advance scouts for a human army that could invade their world. This would delay the dynasty's ultimate plan which seems to be genocide for all human races of all Earths.

Our heroes are not the only human beings on Earth 1-1-3.

After a long hiatus, there's another incarnation of Conrad Bennish. Although we see him, he can't see anyone. Looks like the claim that Kromaggs enjoy eating human eyes is not purely propaganda.

The most significant human character they meet is a sad and lonely woman named Mary, hauntingly portrayed by Una Damon. She tells them a lot of what they have already figured out. For instance, the Kromaggs have mastered pinpoint control of gravitational forces, which enables them not only to power their ships but also to contain prisoners—they can keep you stuck against a wall like a bug on fly-paper.

Mary is the interpreter for the Kromaggs. She says that because they refuse to learn a Homo sapien tongue, she and her masters communicate telepathically. The story of her life consists of one tragedy. They took her as a child to the Kromagg world where she was tormented and brought up to serve them.

The Kromaggs want the Sliders to give them the exact coordinates of their home Earth. Our heroes have a tremendous advantage in not knowing the answer, so they can't possibly slip up and give it away.

Rembrandt is subjected to a vision of his father, or an alternate father from some other Earth. Either way, he knows the man is not his father when he mentions Rembrandt's sister. In his world, the Crying Man doesn't have a sister. This scene is chilling because of the nervous way the man continually refers to the Kromaggs as liberators who have humanity's best interests at heart.

Arturo is tricked into talking to a Rembrandt who isn't there. Another prisoner next door fails to cheer him up with stories about Kromagg caviar (the eyes have it) and Arturo isn't convinced that the man is even real.

Wade receives the full, sadistic treatment. She sits in a high revolving chair under hot lights, sweating in fear, as a female voice taunts her about torturing Quinn to death if Wade doesn't tell the

Kromaggs what they want to know. When she keeps repeating that she doesn't know the answers they want, the voice asks if she'd tell if she did know. Wade truthfully answers no, and receives an extra dose of torment.

Reunited with the others, Arturo points out that Quinn must be perceived by the enemy as the most dangerous of them because of his knowledge of sliding. Also, Quinn was the only one of them to actually kill a Kromagg. Rembrandt, Wade, and Arturo agree to attempt an escape even if it costs them their lives, and even if they must proceed without Quinn.

But Quinn is alive and undergoing a far more subtle interview than his companions. In a garden spot on this barren planet, a solarium, Mary befriends him, telling about the world of the Kromaggs where the trees dwarf our redwoods.

He responds by telling her that she can help but she doesn't seem to believe it. But then she slips him a key before he leaves. When the Sliders are reunited, they don't hesitate to try the key. Even if it's a trap they might as well go for it. They see that the man in the cell next to them is real enough: a blind Bennish. He freaks out at the thought that they might escape and calls for the guards. They overcome the first two. Thinking ahead, Quinn disables some of the enemy's sliding equipment so they won't be immediately followed.

Other guards corner them but Mary comes through and zaps the Kromaggs, seeming to be hit herself. She returns the timer/gizmo and has conveniently programmed it to take them to the world in which they were captured.

After the Sliders return to New France, Mary reveals herself as not quite the humanist she seemed to be, although she is fully human and not a Kromagg illusion. One of the Kromaggs is speaking to her in English (so much for refusing to use a human tongue) and boasts of a tracking device's having been implanted in one of the Sliders. The Kromaggs are convinced the Sliders don't know the location of their home Earth. The tracking device will allow them to track the humans on all future journeys, and if they ever reach Quinn's world it will be attacked in force.

What is Mary's reward for this ultimate betrayal of her own species? She is granted one hour of freedom in the garden before returning to her cage. She cries a single tear. What must her life be like?

AS TIME GOES BY

Written by Steve Brown
Directed by Richard Compton
Music by Stephen Graziano

GUEST STARS:

Brooke Langton as Daelin Richards
Matthew Flint as Dennis McMillan

WITH:

Charlie O'Connell as Kit Richards
Dennys Payamps as Gloria Sanchez
Eli Gabay as La Migra
Mina E. Mina as Judge Estavez
Lori Triolo as La Padrona
Gary Rousseau as Jailer
James Crescenzo as Head Guard
Francisco Trujillo as El Padron
Dee Jay Jackson as Baliff

Watching this season finale of *Sliders* reminded me of history courses I took in college. Most of the Founding Fathers would have been horrified to see the United States acquire colonies of exactly the same sort that formed the backbone of the British imperial system. In the world of "As Time Goes By," the consequences of real history are reversed by the simple expedient of Spain's having won all the military victories required to control the continent.

The adventure begins with the Sliders' encountering a new kind of alien: Canadians. The fans are given an inside joke when a Canuck says, "Kinda nippy out here, eh? Reminds me of Vancouver."

Then something more unusual is noticed. All the signs are in Spanish. Only Spanish. A bad sign for English-speaking people.

Right on cue, immigration officers raid the group. Everyone is captured except Quinn. Arturo, Rembrandt, and Wade are dragged off to court, where they are sentenced to be deported to Canada.

I love this episode.

Quinn hides in the backyard of a mansion where, with the kind of luck for which the show is famous, he encounters this world's alternate of a childhood sweetheart, Daelin. She's not one of the few wealthy Norteamericanos who hobnob with the Castilian aristocracy. She's a maid. She remembers her Quinn, who moved away in high school, and naturally transfers affection to our Quinn. Through her, he is able to make contact with her brother, who is an outlaw.

There's another man in her life: one of those annoying husbands that old girlfriends pick up. This husband's name is Dennis, and he turns out to be an informant. Daelin's brother goes to all sorts of trouble to free Wade, Arturo, and Rembrandt, along with all the other immigrants on the deportation bus. The interfering husband ruins the whole plan by tipping off the authorities so that no sooner are the people freed from the bus than they're being rounded up again. Dennis is a menace.

Despite their failure to improve conditions in Spanish World, they don't have to go to Canada because it's time to slide again. Quinn is distressed that he can't convince Daelin to slide with him.

I spent so much time on the last world's alternate history premise that I can be more succinct about the next world's differences from ours. The 49ers are known as the Lions.

Back to the drama. Having found Daelin again, Quinn finds it difficult to let go. O'Connell's expressive face let's us know he's got it bad. In this world, he encounters another Quinn, who is emotionally stuck on the Daelin here. This Quinn is at the University of Washington. More trouble: Daelin is in an abusive relationship with an alternate Dennis. This guy seems to have serious problems, so naturally he winds up with the girl.

Quinn helps her and a young daughter out of the domestic pressure-cooker and plays matchmaker between her and Quinn #2. He's not going to ask a mother with a young child to slide with him, so he settles on the next-best thing.

Speaking of sliding, there's one more trip in this busy episode. This one is based on Stephen Hawking's theory that time may run backwards in some dimensions. I've never done the research, but I'll bet the first fictional use of this notion did not precede the invention of movies, because running film backwards seems such an obvious source of inspiration.

They go from cell to courtroom, where they were/are convicted of murdering Daelin; to the scene of the crime where they witness not her murder but an attempted murder. On the theory that even Quinn's luck must eventually run out, this Daelin didn't/doesn't recognize her old friend.

One guess about the man with whom she's involved. But this time he's not a creep. Law of averages.

The Sliders prevent the murder. No one in Backwards World realizes this. In fact, Daelin is unhappy over what she believes to have happened. Ditto for Dennis, who is an undercover cop here. She's his partner and fiancé. With enough possible universes, a miserably unhappy couple finally gets it right. Too bad it has to be in a world where the clocks run backwards.

Before this last segment rewinds itself, the whole Earth is shown to be reversed and...there's a gigantic tear in the sky.

Best line is Arturo thundering to Quinn: "You have ripped the fabric of time."

Second best line is Quinn quoting Wade: "Wow!"

The timer can't be expected to function in a world where everything is ass-backwards. Is this the end of our heroes, caught in a temporal loop inside a formula cop story?

Nope. They are saved when the vortex appears behind them and sucks them up like a vacuum cleaner. Wow.

END OF SECOND SEASON

PART FIVE:
THIRD SEASON

"What if you could find a portal to a parallel universe? What if you could slide into a thousand different worlds—where it's the same year and you're the same person, but everything else is different?

And what if you can't find your way home?" SSSSSSllllllliiiiiiiiiiii-iiideeeeeeeeeeeeRRRRRRRSSSSSS

After the first two seasons were shot in and around Vancouver, with some establishing material in San Francisco, the third season moved to Hollywood. The co-executive chores had already gone to Tony Blake and Paul Jackson, who first started being noticed by fans for their scripts in the second season (e.g., "Love Gods" and "Gillian of the Spirits"). The executive producer was a famous name in Hollywood, David Peckinpah. Tormé and Weiss continued to be involved: a script by Tormé is the high-water mark of the third season, and maybe the whole series.

The advantages of the move included a more expensive look and the opportunity to use L.A. locations (which meant the poor timer had to be messed with again so that the Sliders could find themselves in other places than old San Francisco). The disadvantage was the decreasing emphasis on alternate history and an increase in, well, Brad Linaweaver logic. Of course, there had already been a few we-are-in-an-impossible-world moments before the third season, but they did not dominate the series. *Sliders* was primarily a science-fiction show up to this point. Now there was more fantasy, a predictable result of moving to Hollywood, some might say.

DOUBLE CROSS

Written by Tony Blake and Paul Jackson
Directed by Richard Compton
Music by Stephen Graziano

GUEST STARS:
Zoe McLellan as Logan St. Clair
Michael Bryan French as Adrian Fayne
Mari Morrow as Monique
Lester Barrie as Diggs
Diana Castle as Mrs. Arturo

WITH:
Warren Sweeney as Vendor
Kris Iyer as Maitre D'
Monte Perlin as Motorcycle Guard
Charles Noland as Desk Clerk
Skip Stellrecht as Guard #1
Michael Marich as Guard #2
David L. Nelson as Mike
Michael Krawic as Hobo
Gerry Del Sol as Passenger

For the first time since "Eggheads" and "Into the Mystic," the Sliders arrive in an America that already knows about sliding. "Post-Traumatic Slide Syndrome" is about introducing the concept to the world.

In San Angeles, a well-known company has been pushing the

concept for years but has been unable to work out the bugs. The project is headed by a woman named Logan St. Clair, probably the best villain of the series.

They enter S.A. (something familiar about those initials) and find themselves in a tunnel. Here comes a train. A TRAIN! They run for it but Rembrandt gets his foot stuck in the damned track.

In an excellent scene, the other Sliders refuse to abandon their friend, but continue trying to free him up to the last second. The Sliders are ready to end it all here and now rather than abandon Rembrandt. They are saved at the last possible second by the train's coming to a halt, its headlight dimming, as a female PA informs them: "Attention, please. This is the daily ten o'clock power blackout for sector forty-seven. Service will resume in thirty minutes. Thank you."

Now Rembrandt can pop his foot out of his boot. Wouldn't you know it?

On the city streets, they notice skateboards, bikes, and rickshaws. Wade wonders if they've reached a world that's banned gas-powered vehicles. Rembrandt soon discovers there may be more serious bans in the place when he attempts ordering a hot dog with chili and cheese. The street vendor looks at him as if he's nuts. The only food the vendor has for sale is a gruel called Geomash. It comes in two flavors: green and yellow.

Rembrandt's close call with the train is offset by some serious good luck. A gorgeous babe approaches and asks if he's Rembrandt Brown. Her name is Monique. There's a law that only beautiful women are allowed to call themselves Monique. (That's not from the episode. I made it up.)

She's a fan of this world's Crying Man and read that he's doing a European tour. Ah, the advantages of hitting town when your double is out of town. She flatters Remmy outrageously and he eats it all up. She's rich. She offers to fly him to L.A. in her private jet where they'll have some fun. Naturally, he goes off with her before he finds out what kind of world this is. Now what man would do something like that? Let's see a show of, er, hands.

Meanwhile, the street vendor reports the Sliders to motorcycle guards for the unspeakable crime of ordering a hot dog. Gee whiz, a street vendor wouldn't rat you out in Nazi Germany or Soviet Russia, but California is something else again.

The Sliders must visit shoe stores a lot. With all the running they do, it must be kind of hard on the soles. The motorcyclists chase them and they haul ass. Finally, they're cornered in an alley. The lead cyclist pulls off her helmet, revealing this world's number-one, intelligent, knock-out, mad-scientist doll, Logan St. Clair. "Sliders!" she calls out. That gets their attention.

The presence of Maximillian Arturo gets her attention. She tells him that his double in this world died two nights ago as a result of his being the first to try a slide. Logan wants to know if they have encountered doubles in all the worlds they visit.

Quinn replies, "Not always." The irony is not lost on us later.

Conveniently, Logan's lab contains a biothermal security scanner that reads a person's unique body-heat pattern. A handy household item for anyone who regularly receives Sliders as guests.

Logan learns that Quinn Mallory is a male version of herself. She decides that it might be expedient to prevent Quinn's sliding anytime soon. She has plans for him.

As so often happens, Arturo spends a bit more time thinking about the people they meet than do his traveling companions. He has encountered many versions of himself, some outright villains, but nowhere in all his travels has he come across a stupid Arturo. He doubts that any version of himself would slide without running tests first.

Logan has promised Quinn to help get them home. The idea is certainly feasible. At least they're in a place with a brand new sliding machine. Quinn and Logan working together ought to produce good scientific results. They've never really had an opportunity of this sort. Quinn wants to believe they've found a new friend, but Arturo can't shake his suspicions.

Wade learns a lot about this world jsut from staying in her hotel room. Five-minute power blackouts are scheduled every three hours. Bathing is limited to two minutes. It's even requested that guests shower together to conserve resources.

When Arturo finds out that Logan was having an affair with his double in this world—she'd earlier tried to make him think she hardly knew the man—it is another blow to her veracity. Arturo shares his discovery with Wade.

A happier man at the moment is one Rembrandt Brown, who is enjoying all the extra features of Monique's Malibu beach house, complete with hot tub (a better way of checking out unique body-heat patterns). Judicious television editing and apparel suggests that he has scored big time.

Then he runs into a problem, but it seems to be far more than a wrinkle for this world's Rembrandt to sort out. She's turned a whole room into a shrine for the Crying Man. Rembrandt #2 never replied to her hundreds of letters except via his lawyer. The revelation that Monique expects to marry the Crying Man would cause consternation under normal circumstances. Except that this Rembrandt is a Slider.

He hasn't even left a problem for this world's Rembrandt because the other guy is currently being seen by zillions of fans in Europe, a perfect alibi. Only a pregnancy could cause her Rembrandt serious problems. Imagine the court case. Genetic testing could prove that Monique's baby is the Crying Tot. However did he do it?

Back at the lab, we see where some of the extra power that the government works so hard to conserve goes. As Logan ups the amperage to increase the size of her vortex, she overdoes it and is almost sucked in. Quinn saves her. He also saves his timer/gizmo from being pulled in. Quinn can't understand why she needs so much power.

Quinn doesn't like the answer he finds. Logan St. Clair intends to steal resources from other Earths, a truly clever idea . . . and bad to the bone. When he learns the truth, he turns against her and sabotages her equipment.

Rembrandt is only too happy to rejoin his friends. Arturo is happy to be vindicated about Logan. Wade is happy to leave behind a world that doesn't provide enough hot water. Quinn is happiest of all to escape a female villain who is this episode's Quinn #2.

They slide, but the adventure isn't over by a long shot. Logan is a fast learner. She slides after them and attempts to abduct Quinn. Quinn hasn't changed his mind and wants no part in helping her to rape the universe. Even if this means he'll never get home, he sticks to his guns.

Speaking of guns, Logan St. Clair has brought one. I wish the Sliders had their very own gun. They could have picked one up back in "The Good, the Bad, and the Wealthy." Is that so wrong? Anyway, Logan threatens Wade with the gun.

The villainess knows how Quinn feels about her by this time. He'd rather strangle her than shoot her. As it is, Quinn defeats her by outsmarting her. He creates a gateway using her timer and then tosses her timer into it, forcing her to dive after it, an act that succeeds in sucking her into the vortex.

Here comes a pun. In the best shot of the show, Logan fires at Wade, but the bullet is grabbed by the suction before it reaches its target and disappears into the wormhole. Not very likely, but it looks cool.

RULES OF THE GAME

Written by Josef Anderson
Directed by Oscar L. Costo
Music by Danny Lux

GUEST STARS:
Laurie Fortier as Nicky
Joshua Malina as Egghead

The show bible says the following about this show: "Our Sliders land in a world where they are inadvertently mistaken for an elite team that is competing in a real-life ultimate endurance game where androids and terminator-type machines exist and rule a playing field that changes from level to level, posing more threats and

danger with each advancement. It's kill or be killed and once the game begins, the Sliders have no choice but to compete in order to survive."

The teaser: They slide onto a plane in flight. This surprises them because they have always come to rest on terra firma up to this moment in their adventures. Suddenly the plane seems to be crashing. The other passengers seem to be going through the motions instead of losing it as they face their doom.

The Sliders do more than go through the motions. Especially when they notice an anomaly. No one is in the cockpit. Arturo and Quinn know something about flying, and they do their best. Rembrandt and Wade join hands. The Sliders all look at each other for what they imagine is the last time.

However, their farewells are premature. The whole event was a simulation. They've been on a ride a lot meaner than anything at Universal Studios Hollywood.

In short order, they find out they're part of a group slated to play in a brutal game. As everyone departs the hangar containing the Plane Ride from Hell, Arturo suggests they simply wait out this nonsense until they slide. They have plentiful supplies on the Plane

Ride and it's only thirty-eight hours to go. When the interior of the hangar starts heating up, they realize that their behavior had been anticipated by the designers of the game. They have only moments to grab supplies and get outside before the building bursts into flame. They cut it so close that Quinn's tennis shoes begin to melt.

So far it seems as if I'm doing a complete summary, doesn't it? Now we reach the video-game situation.

They are a team playing a lethal game. They encounter talking stone gnomes and giant mechanical spiders called "mechspiders." But mostly, they encounter androids that shoot at them. They shoot back. They meet another player named Nicky, a pleasant housewife driven to risk her life in the pursuit of worldly rewards. She's zapped. As she dies, she whispers a memorable line: "See you at the beach."

The Sliders win. You can tell because they survive. But no one told them the final score. For this episode, Arturo is struck temporarily blind. He recovers his sight in time for the slide.

DEAD MAN SLIDING

Written by Nan Hagan
Directed by Richard Compton
Music by Stephen Graziano

GUEST STARS:
Perrey Reeves as Taryn Miller
Fredric Lane as Phil
Lawrence Hilton-Jacobs as Lawrence Hilton-Jacobs
Don Most as Skip Collins
Lisa Rieffel as Deanne Bloch

WITH:
Robert Ditillio as Emcee
Ed Wasser as Studio Guard
Brett Miller as Prison Guard

Intrepid researcher Vanessa Koman notes that this is one of the episodes in which Jerry O'Connell takes off his shirt. Should there ever be a Sliders trivia book, data such as this will be very important.

One of the most natural ideas for science-fiction movies and TV is the game show gone berserk. It's fun when the media exaggerates its own worst tendencies. Ever since the *Sliders* pilot with Rembrandt's trial on *The People's Court*, this show has been conscious of the medium it uses. There's something almost inevitable about the Sliders' reaching a world where the criminal court system has been taken over by the television industry and justice is meted out via game-show thrills. Mob rule (i.e., democracy) is not to be slighted as the audience votes on the verdicts.

This one begins in the world of the main storyline. Logan St. Clair messed around with Quinn's timer/gizmo so that the Sliders may now end up in any part of California. Naturally, the very first place they reach is Hollywood. Will they ever get home? If they can't immediately tell if they are in their San Francisco, what hope do they have as they wander the entire state?

All that Wade knows is that she's in HOLLYWOOD, and she wants to make like a tourist. They have fun until Quinn spots a wallet on Hollywood Boulevard and picks it up, looking for identification and noticing that it contains three hundred dollars.

Right away, they realize this is not their Hollywood. People stop what they're doing to stare in amazement and shock at a man picking up a wallet. He places the wallet back on the street. Hard to believe, but this innocuous act places him in jeopardy again. He didn't pocket it, and maybe he intended to return it to its rightful owner. At any rate, he puts it right back where he found it.

No matter. This must be the season of female fuzz because another young model type turns out to be a cop and starts chasing Quinn. Having gotten the obligatory jog out of the way, the Sliders catch their collective breath. Wade's starhunting reveals a number of unfamiliar names (an opportunity for industry jokes).

They go to the Last Chance Bar (which I'll wager is a wholly owned subsidiary of the Dominion Hotel), where a game show is playing on the tube. The crowd at the bar is really getting into it. The Sliders are given slips of paper in case they wish to bet on the outcome of what they begin to realize is a televised trial.

Before they can place any bets, the female gendarme enters the bar and arrests Quinn. Her name is Taryn. She calls Quinn by his last name. There must be more going on here than the wallet incident.

Quinn isn't dragged off to a conventional jail. Instead, he's hustled off to be a "contestant" on the TV show. According to the rules, a friend is allowed to speak for him as his advocate. Arturo volunteers. The funniest scene ensues when Arturo finds out that he is only qualified because he never went to law school or passed the bar.

A videotape is played of this world's Quinn first mugging a man and then strangling him. Despite the circus atmosphere, Arturo keeps trying to instill a reasonable doubt. He is pelted with popcorn and jeered but presses on. The audience wants a good show. This is L.A., God bless it.

Wade tries to convince Taryn that the Quinn she arrested is not the Quinn she's looking for. When nothing else works, she falls back on the full truth. One thing about telling people about sliding is they sure as hell aren't expecting to hear it.

On TV, in the hot seat, Quinn tells his accuser, the dreaded Skip, all about sliding. The crowd cheers. The entertainment value is way up there. Even Skip is impressed by the inventiveness. The verdict's still guilty.

But there remains one last turn of the screw. His fate now depends on the turn of a wheel, which comes to a stop on #1. Skip opens Door Number One revealing . . . a mini-guillotine.

As Quinn is dragged away, he has a last chance to tell Taryn that he is an innocent man. His words dig deep when he suggests that she's just in it for the money. (There's a Hollywood subtext running through all this, of course. Winners and losers. That's all that matters. Right and wrong are irrelevant. Being found guilty of murder is bad because it makes you a loser.)

The only hope is to find Quinn's double. Wade saves the day with her built-in Quinn detector. She finds Deanne, a girlfriend of Q-ball #2. Wade passes herself off as someone he knocked up. She tells the girl that all she wants from her Quinn is money to get home and then she'll be history. This award-winning performance does the trick. Deanne admits Q2 is hiding out at Deanne's place.

Meanwhile, Taryn was stung by our Quinn's words. She goes to see him and asks that he take off his shirt. A close examination fails to detect a scar that her world's Quinn received when he was knifed in a bar fight.

All that remains is to spin the wheel of the Plot Machine. Arturo, with his sense of objectivity, has argued that this society's method of dealing with criminals offers some benefits in terms of a lower crime rate, it is no more immune to the slow grinding of bureaucracy than any other. Although Wade and Taryn are working together, they can't get through to Network Appeals. But now that Taryn knows for certain that Wade's Quinn is not the right man, she has no intention of allowing his head to fall so that a show's ratings rise.

Taryn arranges for a television van to be in the complex where Quinn will meet his fate. His first reaction to being asked for an interview for the European affiliates is to tell them to shove it . . . until he notices Wade insisting that there's time for one interview. He agrees and climbs into the back of the van, along with Taryn and Wade. Arturo is at the wheel. Rembrandt is on board. Quinn has time to tell Taryn that he misjudged her before they hide him in a false bottom of the van. The final circumstantial touch is tying up Taryn so that when the van is opened, she seems to have been overpowered by the fugitive.

This escape plan would have worked except for the annoying baddie who spots Quinn's hideyhole. Things had to go wrong so this episode could boast the single most exciting slide of the entire series. Step One: Get both the baddie and Taryn off the van so only Sliders remain on board. (Outside the van, Taryn buys them a little more time by brandishing a videotape as if it were Excalibur—a tape proving a worse crime than murder in this society: the TV show is fixed!) Step Two: Our heroes drive in the only direction where they don't see fences or guards, resulting in the one literal cliffhanger of the series. Step Three: The timer shows the slide is less than a minute away. Step Four: A small army of guards rushes them.

When the timer reaches thirteen seconds, Quinn decides it's his lucky number and makes a daring decision. At eight seconds, he sets the example and the others follow: Arturo first and then Wade and Rembrandt, holding hands as they all perform the bravest slide ever, ever, ever. Quinn jumps off the cliff. They jump off the cliff. The guards stop in their tracks, jaws agape. The rule book doesn't cover mass suicide.

The Sliders shout and scream in free fall, but Quinn is still counting. Right before they become part of the scenery rushing up to greet them, the vortex opens. They tumble onto a patch of grass, safe and sound. If they can catch their breath, slow down their heart rates, and turn off the adrenalin, they'll be OK.

A shadowy woman videotapes the Sliders' arrival in the new world. Quinn goes into her house and recovers the tape. When asked how he managed to expedite matters, he says he told the woman that they were aliens who would take her with them back to their world if she didn't fork over the evidence. When asked why the Sliders look alien all of a sudden, Quinn hurries down the street, leaving the others wondering what he's seen. That boy has long legs.

ELECTRIC TWISTER ACID TEST

Written by Scott Smith Miller
Directed by Oscar L. Costo
Music by Stephen Graziano

GUEST STARS:
Corey Feldman as Reed Michener
Julie Benz as Jenny Michener
Bill Bolender as Franklin Michener
Tim Griffin as Jacob
Joshua Cox as Martin
Jordan Blake-Warkol as Caleb

Amazingly, this very next episode also features a scene of Jerry O'Connell's upper torso sans shirt. Guess who made sure that I didn't fail to include this crucial information.

The gateway opens but the Sliders don't arrive in the usual way. They are riding in a bobsled. From ice to sand, they enter a barren landscape where the only greenery is scrub and Joshua trees. The sports angle is maintained when the first person they see in this desert is a kid whose snowboard catches a ride on a small tornado! The kid can't be more than twelve years old and wears goggles. He starts off like he's in control but shortly gets into trouble.

Arturo recognizes that the twister is being generated artificially by an electrical current. Quinn runs over to help and tackles the boy, pulling him out of danger. Instead of expressing gratitude, the kid runs off and literally vanishes into thin air before their eyes.

The mysteries mount up. Arturo counts four tornadoes within one hour. When Quinn examines his timer, it's going haywire. He can't tell how long it will be to the next slide. Although they're thirsty, they don't dare drink from the only water they find in a watering hole because of all the dead critters surrounding it like grotesque decorations.

Rembrandt thinks the water must be poisoned but that's not the real danger. Quinn tosses metal into the water and the liquid crackles and buzzes. The surface of the planet is electrically charged.

Wade finds a small farm community off in the distance that seems unravaged by the ubiquitous twisters. They head for it. As they draw near, Quinn announces the timer is stabilizing. Lodestones in the surrounding area are the reason they can take refuge from the electrical weirdness.

They spot a dead man. The corpse is on display in old-fashioned wooden stocks. A posted warning reads: OUTCASTS CAUGHT RAIDING WILL BE EXECUTED. Ignorance of the rules may be no excuse but these are four hungry, thirsty, exhausted explorers who help themselves to supplies inside the barn.

A woman named Jenny finds them and asks if they are from Reed's camp. They admit they're strangers in need of help. The conversation is interrupted by the sound of a tornado. Jenny is calm. They look outside and witness an upside-down twister in the distance, much larger than any of the others. Flashes of lightning dance around it. Arturo is as calm as Jenny, convinced that the lodestones will protect them from the electrically charged wind storm.

Wade is first to question the theory she's heard from so many when she observes the tornado is getting closer. Jenny is shocked by the sight. They close up the barn as tightly as possible and prepare to weather the storm.

Quinn gives them an important clue about what's happening: "There's nothing electrical inside the lodestone to attract it." All the Sliders are struck by the same thought as if by a lightning bolt. They are among folk who live as if there had never been a Thomas Edison or Henry Ford. Rembrandt says that the timer is a magnet for the tornado.

Jenny doesn't want harm to come to these good-natured strangers and warns them not to let her father see their timer/gizmo. Right on cue, her father makes an appearance. His name is Franklin and he wears a mighty scowl. In an awful lot of fiction, fathers of beautiful daughters are a psychotic lot. Daddy wastes no time accusing our heroes of stealing food and bringing tornadoes.

Fortunately, executions are always postponed when there's information to be pumped out of prisoners. The Elders don't believe the story of sliding; and they believe that the strangers can tell them the locations of the outcast community.

Some of the men of the community, the ones with eyes in their heads, think it would be a sin to banish Wade, who is of child bearing age. Right before they take her and place her under the care of Jenny, Quinn promises he'll find a way back if Wade can recover the timer.

The men are taken to a desolate region where they are to be banished. As they bump along on the uncomfortable wagon ride, Arturo notes that Franklin is no simple bumpkin. The man was capable of dismantling the timer with some skill. Another mystery to solve.

Rembrandt, Arturo, and Quinn are left in the middle of nowhere without food or water. At least they don't have to deal with twisters right away. Instead, there's a medium-sized sandstorm.

The boy Quinn rescued earlier finally shows some gratitude. His name is Caleb and he finds them, offering his help. He is dressed desert nomad style and knows his way around a sand dune. He leads them to an underground compound lit by solar-powered lamps. They meet Reed, leader of the outcasts. Why, the man is Franklin's son. All in the family...

In the community proper, Wade dresses like Jenny and works like Jenny. The clothing seems an odd cross between Amish dress and threads dug out of a wardrobe department for old westerns. Wade learns that Franklin is the patriarch because he's the one who discovered that lodestones are protections against the twisters. Jenny tells Wade that the leader of the outcasts is her brother. Wade returns the favor by showing Jenny how to stand up for herself in a male-dominated society.

Jenny offers to help Wade deliver supplies to her banished friends. Foolishly, they lead Franklin and some of his men to their location. Wade and Jenny are easily detained but Caleb is not so easy to capture. The kid runs into the tunnel, followed by two of the men.

Dear Old Dad promises to make an example of his daughter and her friend. Down in the bunker, Quinn explains the timer/gizmo to the leader and how it will only work in reverse-polarity areas. Reed assures Quinn that despite his father's Luddite rhetoric, the man remains a scientist who would never really destroy a piece of advanced technology. Franklin was head of a big government research project in the '60s. Experimenting with electromagnetic dynamos inadvertently created Tornado World.

Jenny gets in touch with inner feelings and empowers herself. Her husband, Jacob, relents on part of the shunning...but not all. She knees him in the groin! Amazing. She helps Wade regain the timer/gizmo. All well and good. But Franklin catches Wade, holding a pitchfork to her throat.

Back in the science-fiction department, Arturo discovers a way to create an electrical perimeter that will provide the same protection as the lodestones, thus allowing them to slide. Now all they have to do is get everyone together in time.

Quinn rescues Wade from more problems. Now the community is punishing Wade by dunking her. All that's missing is a scene where they hang her, then take her down and behead her, then burn the remains and scatter the ashes.

Despite all his vile behavior, Franklin still wakes up and smells the coffee when he has a showdown with his son. Reed is stern with his old man, even threatening to kill him. Franklin takes the blame for having created Tornado World and then having lied about it so that he could construct this rather peculiar society. Now the old man says he'll try to make good by finding a way to eliminate the tornado threat. Maybe he'll institute a fair and just society. Sure he will.

Arturo succeeds in eliminating and normalizing the area's magnetic field. Reversing the polarity of the zone has one downside: attracting twisters. The small ones merge into the Moby Dick of all twisters. Or they would have except the special effects seem to run out of steam. The Sliders get out of there while the getting's good.

THE GUARDIAN

Written by Tracy Tormé
Directed by Adam Nimoy
Music by Danny Lox

GUEST STARS:

Philip Van Dyke as Young Quinn
Leslie Horan as Heather Hanley
Linda Henning as Mrs. Mallory
Meadow Sisto as Ambrosia

WITH:

Marty York as Brady Oaks
Timothy Wiley as Rex Crandell
Robert Winley as Bull
John Kendall as Bartender
John Colton as Priest

If not for the pilot, this would be my favorite episode of *Sliders*. As such, I insist on devoting as much space in this guide as necessary to do it justice.

"The Guardian" does everything right. Tracy Tormé deserves kudos for the script. Many stories have explored the idea of what it would mean to go back and meet your childhood self, but the special few succeed in touching the secret places where we bottle up our regrets and lost hopes. "The Guardian" is one of these.

Science fiction provides a modern version of this oldest of wishes made flesh. Is there anyone alive who wouldn't share the hard-won wisdom of hindsight with their childhood self? Doesn't every parent confront this daily, wishing to save children from experiences they so desperately need to grow into mature men and women?

And then there is the other direction to be considered: the things we learn when young, the bittersweet truths of childhood that we stupidly forget as we become adults, convinced that maturity means amnesia. The only adult who has anything worth teaching a child is an adult who can also learn from a child. Although the words come easily, the reality is that an adult must first believe a child has rights. In a world where most adults don't even believe in the rights of other adults, or even themselves, the challenge of teaching something to a child is the most difficult thing in the world: it involves learning from your mistakes.

Tormé said in his interview, "All the themes in 'The Guardian' were happening in my real life at the time." (Mel Tormé was very ill.) "There was even a night my wife and I went out to watch a meteor shower in the desert with some friends, and he was at the lowest ebb at that point. I had just written the scene which was an added scene to the piece where Quinn and his younger self go out to look at the stars ... It was the theme of father and son, and not saying all the things you wanted to say and now it's too late and you may never have another opportunity to say them."

The story begins with Arturo's going to a doctor's office, but this is nothing like the time Rembrandt went to the psychiatrist in search of a sympathetic ear. We suspect something very serious is happening. Arturo is not grim or angry. After his thorough examination, his face shows something we don't expect to see from that large and joyful soul: a sense of resignation. Arturo is tired. Arturo is in pain.

The sun is bright on the street outside as if to mock the darkness the whirring technologies have probed inside the big man who is now slumped against a wall. A private man does not wish to share visions of the end with those who love him. He can barely express his feelings at the best of times. His life is subtle and indirect, his manner of approval more the art of a withheld criticism. He doesn't know why he is this way. But the specter of death forces him to feel. And the last thing in the world he wants to do is share the bitterness and dread and emptiness with someone who truly cares about him.

Someone like Quinn Mallory, his opposite in all kinds of little things that suddenly seem unimportant. Quinn in his twenties, who could live a hundred years and never know for one hour, one minute, the kind of regrets that Arturo carries. Quinn, who not only will never be the kind of adult Arturo cannot help being, but will not even suffer the adult miseries of Wade or Rembrandt. Quinn, whom Arturo loves more than he loves himself because the universe loves the lad so much it will give up its deepest secrets to his questing mind easily, with little fuss.

The blessed ones never know why others look upon them as something unobtainable. Now a man who feels he is looking at as true a son as he will ever have must tell that son he's dying from an incurable disease. He doesn't know how long he has, but he does know one thing: "The end will be cruel, and without dignity."

There, it is said. The words expelled as if they were secret toxins eating away at life and happiness. Now Arturo must speak empty words, foolish words, about leaving his friends, his family of Quinn and Wade and Rembrandt. He talks of having a private adventure but Quinn sees through him, and cannot stand the idea of the big, hearty, deeply human man who is Maximillian Arturo crawling into some corner to sicken and weaken and die...alone. The worst death. The lonely death.

Youth bursts out of Quinn. He can't keep it bottled up. He will have nothing to do with unspoken feelings by which adults build their solitary prisons. "Go then!" he cries, his voice breaking. Even as he accuses the older man of walking out on him, they both understand the unspoken truth: Quinn will be lonely without Arturo.

Arturo knows that if he once turns and looks into that face, he will not die alone. He thinks it noble to keep his own counsel when everything has turned to ashes. But death is such a poor substitute for a friend. God help him, he cannot resist. He turns and is lost, falling into the blue sky and blue eyes, and knowing that soon he will be falling into a blue tunnel.

Quinn insists that they all need Arturo, unaware of how true his words are this time. Soon he will need Arturo more than he has ever needed him before. He will need the man who is the closest to being his lifelong father to help him, to guide him, as he tries to deal with an experience rare for him...something he thought was buried long ago in a young boy's obsession with work: the pain of a childhood that surpasses any of Arturo's midnight wanderings of the soul. There is no room for drab adult torments in one whose memories of childhood are as vivid as if they were yesterday.

Quinn will soon witness himself as the child who built a fortress out of his own mind and banished himself into its deepest recesses. He worked hard to make himself into the loneliest person in the universe.

Perhaps no surprise, then, that with a mind the size of an exploding galaxy, Quinn would not stay forever in his basement dungeon. But instead of walking away from it, body and soul, Quinn found a way to leave all the basements of all lost childhoods. He found the way to slide.

This time his friends join him in a San Francisco of long ago, at a funeral ceremony where his father is laid to rest too soon, and his shaken mother stands by the graveside. She is younger but already experiences the emptiness working away at her, leeching the years out of her. Holding her hand, but not touching, never really touching again, is the young Quinn Mallory watching the universe prove itself small and narrow and stupid.

The universe that let him down and so now must be conquered. The universe that will be so much more forgiving and cooperative than any living soul . . . until Quinn finds Wade Welles with an ocean of love to give, and Rembrandt Brown with an ocean of loyalty and friendship. And then there's the replacement for the man in the graveyard, the professor who now threatens to follow Quinn's real father into the tomb.

Even in the torrent of emotion, Quinn must think. He is all about thinking. Nor will Arturo roll over and die when there is a problem to be solved. He, too, must think.

Rembrandt poses the question on his and Wade's mind: "I thought we couldn't travel back in time, only to parallel worlds, but here we are twelve years ago."

Arturo and Quinn take turns explaining. It's good to explain. Good to use human reason and stay sane. This Earth must revolve  around the sun at the same rate as ours, but spin more quickly on its axis.

Quinn amplifies: "It's 1996, but from our perspective, events are occurring as they did a decade ago."

Never did it occur to Quinn that sliding would give him a second chance. A second chance. He must leave his friends, now, and run, fly, to seize that second chance that the gods in their mercy, or malice, have seen fit to offer him.

Arturo, from the moment of deciding to slide again, made a resolution that he will keep as if every day were New Year's Day. He will live life to the fullest. Here and now, he can attend once again a Mozart concert that moved him so many years ago. He rents a Bentley and takes his young friends for a joy ride. He goes to a biker bar and speaks poetry to an inviting woman and then commits the unpardonable sin of defending himself successfully. He invents Bungee jumping, and to his amazement, enjoys both it and the spectacle of Rembrandt and Wade's straining every muscle to pull him back up to the bridge. He's introduced to American football by Rembrandt, who is thrilled to see one of Joe Montana's best games again, fresh and new, even if the Crying Man knows the score.

But while Arturo is savoring life, and enjoying the company of his sliding companions perhaps as never before, he'll not fail to notice what's happening. Quinn has given him back his life but now takes risks with his own life, times two.

Quinn longs to reach out to his mother in a time before he put her through so much hell. It's not that the boy blames her for his father's death, but as Quinn is able to explain to her in the role of a new-found friend, the boy can dump on her and she will still love him. In the words of the Southern writer, Ward Moore, Quinn longs to touch the fabric of the past. He begins by averting the truly terrible thing that drove a wedge between his mother and him shortly after the death of his father. She left the gate open, and the boy's dog got out and was never seen again.

To lose a dog when you've just lost your father...there is no word in the English language to describe how that would feel to a boy. Or to describe the feelings of his poor mother, who is convinced that she can't do anything right. But adult Quinn averts the disaster of losing the dog. He intends to avert others.

The playground the next day is the scene of a cruel beating Quinn receives from not one, but a collection of bullies. They hate him for his intelligence. They know he has no father, no brother...only a doting mother. They can punish him for their failures, and one's dyslexia.

Except this time everything is different. The Guardian has come. More terrifying to bullies than all the big brothers in the world, for all six feet and five inches of Quinn's trim, hard body—with lean swimmer muscles and a long reach for his fists—is an avenging fury come to visit judgment. His anger is not the anger of an adult simply trying to prevent kids from fighting. This anger burns for justice in the world of boys where there is no justice but only the pack, and rich harvests for the rare evil ones who learn to master the pack.

He doesn't hurt the bullies but he frightens them. Not enough to throw them off the scent of their quarry, but to make them cautious the next time they gather to make young Quinn bleed.

Older Quinn is starting to make dominoes fall and Arturo decides he must speak to his friend. "Suppose your double was meant to experience the same pain you did in order to become the Quinn he's meant to be—the Quinn you are!" To what extent was Quinn's suffering responsible for his becoming the greatest genius of his generation, Edison and Einstein and Dirac rolled up in one package? Has Quinn the right to take that away from his other self?

Quinn wonders what right he has to leave this boy alone to his torture. While listening to Arturo, he allows the boy to be beaten at school without interfering.

Quinn has become the overly protective father of . . . himself, a patriarchy of one. He visits his mother's house more often, in the guise of Jim (sounds like Quinn). There is something familiar about his face but she can't place it. She will remember as her boy grows up, stretching out like a tree to touch the sky, and then that face from her past will return.

As Jim, he is seeing more of Heather, the young teacher he had a crush on. Now he can take her out. They talk not of her or him, but of young Quinn. She wonders how he knows so much about the boy. She cares about young Quinn. Any teacher knows how smart he is. Part of his social problem is that he skips grades and is then the smallest runt in the class.

Finally, Older Quinn can't stay away from . . . himself. He opens a universe of possibilities to young Quinn. They talk about Mom. They also talk about bullies. Older Quinn has to leave soon but not before he alters history one last time. A terrible thing will happen on Friday afternoon, shortly before it's time to slide. There is only a little time left.

As Quinn teaches the boy how to defend himself with boxing, there is a sea change in Arturo. In a scene to parallel the opening of the show, Arturo tells Quinn he supports him in teaching the boy basic defense, like a grandfather who gives his long-desired approval to a son about the rearing of a grandson.

Rembrandt also supports Quinn's choice, leaving Wade to question this fundamental ritual of the Male Lodge. She is hardly strident about it, but with her empathy and natural kindness, she can never appreciate the male's need to prove himself a man. The core tension between all fathers and all sons remains a mystery to her deeply feminine soul.

The night before the terrible Friday, the two Quinns sit out on the porch together and watch the stars. Quinn gives a new thought to the boy. "Did you know we're all made of stardust? You, me, your father, everyone.... You can't actually look up into the heavens and see your Dad ... but one day, his physical essence will be blown into space ... yours and mine, too ... and together, we'll form new stars."

They both agree that's really cool, in one of Tormé's best passages of writing.

Comes the terrible day, Quinn's friends have completely misunderstood the situation he has worked so hard to avert. Young Quinn begins to confront the bullies with a baseball bat, but then drops it. He stands up for himself using the boxing the Guardian has taught him.

In our Quinn's history, he stood up for himself with the baseball bat, permanently crippling one of the other boys. He's felt guilty ever since, but we may also conclude the incident of the bat only did more to leave Quinn a loner. He was so alone that what saved him was that curiosity finally became a stronger force than rage, allowing him to become the remarkable man whom Arturo and Rembrandt and Wade can't help but love.

If I happened to be the kind of guy who cries because of a well-crafted drama—which, of course, I'm not—I'd puddle up over this one. The moisture on my face has nothing to do with the show.

I have something in my eye.

Note: The Sliders find an isolated street from which to depart but Heather comes upon Quinn before he enters the shimmering vortex. She calls him Jim. Right before he leaves, he says his name is Quinn. She knew the kid was smart. This is the true sense of wonder that makes good science fiction.

THE DREAM MASTERS

Teleplay by Melinda Snodgrass
Story by Scott Smith Miller and Melinda Snodgrass
Directed by Jefery Levy
Music by Danny Lux

GUEST STARS:

Zack Ward as Gerald Thomas
Katherine LaNasa as Dr. Olivia Lujan
Michael Des Barres as Vincent Cardoza
Rodney Eastman as Byron
J. Steven Smith as Henry
Lester Barrie as Diggs

WITH:

Symba Smith as Officer Weber
Kenneth Johnson as Skater

To go from a high-water mark like "The Guardian" to the bottom of the septic tank is enough to make a fellow want to turn in his scuba gear. Having drowned that metaphor, I'll move on. I promised when trashing "El Sid" that I'd confess to what I believe qualifies as the worst of the episodes I watched to do this book. When Quinn says that you can't run away from a dream—conveniently forgetting Wade did just that in "Obsession"—I started arguing with the TV set, always a bad sign.

This is another one that will require more space than usual. Maybe it's unfair to choose "The Dream Masters" when there's an episode up ahead that I'm certain would win a poll of viewers as the Grand Turkey Gobbler, an episode that burns me up. Objectively, "The Fire Within" is more than a dumb episode of *Sliders*; it qualifies as one of the dumbest episodes of any TV show ever. Five minutes into the thing, however, the viewer has no expectations. Because "The Dream Masters" had some potential, its failure is inexcusable.

There's nothing wrong with the idea of invading people's dreams. Nor can the acting be faulted. Everyone turns in the usual professional job. Sabrina Lloyd matches many a horror heroine in her portrayal of stark terror. She deserves to be made an honorary Scream Princess. The primary villain is played by Zack Ward with a twitchy intensity that can't be faulted. The technical side of the production is OK. The nightmare sequences are well put together and the effects are good.

So what's the problem? Only that the script sucks. There's nowhere else to place the blame. The idea that it took two writers to come up with something this lame is not encouraging.

I even wanted to like the writing because I know that Melinda Snodgrass is capable of good work. Friends will verify that I praised a script she did for *Star Trek: The Next Generation* because it demonstrated the value of individualism through the character of Data. I don't pretend to have an explanation for what went wrong with this *Sliders* story except to say that it went terribly wrong.

On a pleasant, sunny afternoon, the Sliders arrive at the Santa Monica pier. They are dressed in festive party clothes and the dialogue is charming. They've been enjoying a California that could be mistaken for New Orleans. A nice idea. The French Quarter would be improved by a locale free of humidity.

They are all relaxed and happy. Wade dabs at lipstick on Quinn's face. Looks like Rembrandt wasn't the only one to find himself a girl on the last world. Wade seems to speak for all of them when she says she needs to catch up on her sleep.

Enter trouble. We've seen a sign banning bikes from the boardwalk. Along comes a geeky looking guy on a bike who nearly hits Quinn. A big guy on roller skates is not as fortunate. He collides with the biker, knocking him down.

The skater is rightly indignant until the biker takes off his helmet. The moment the skater recognizes the face he is stricken with terror and offers to do anything to make amends. The bike rider takes the other man up on his offer.

He tells the poor guy to drop dead. The dangerous nerd reveals a pentagram on his palm and slaps the other man on the cheek. The occult symbol appears on the skater's face and then vanishes. The skater promptly has a heart attack and dies.

While all this is going on, the Sliders try to help the dying man. Only Wade really seems to pick up on the bad vibes, exchanging nervous glances with this week's guest villain, who's name they will soon learn is Gerald Thomas.

A female cop named Weber at first seems ready to do her duty until she sees the cause of the trouble is Gerald. Then she switches from asking for an ambulance to a meat wagon. She reports the dead skater as a suicide. When the Sliders try to give their complete stories, they are brushed off. The officer is scared to death of the man with the pentagram and warns the others to lay off.

Gerald saunters over and begins making moves on Wade. She's scared of him but not scared enough to put up with his telling her that he can't wait to sleep with her. Wade punches him a good one. Gerald tells Wade that he'll see her in her dreams.

The Sliders go to a bar. Wade argues with Arturo. She thinks something creepy happened. Arturo is yet to be convinced. The bartender overhears them and provides a name for their pain: the Dream Masters. He lost his last cocktail waitress to one but won't go into further detail. Then Wade sees the creep looking at her but when she tells the others... the Dream Master isn't there.

Now things start to get dumb. First, Rembrandt tells Wade that she needs some sleep. When Wade wisely says she's not going to sleep, Arturo jumps in to say that she can't possibly believe this spooky stuff.

How many weird worlds have they visited? What did they just see? What was the officer afraid of?

After Wade and Arturo go up to the room (where I'm sure Arturo could think of some way to help Wade keep awake) Rembrandt asks an intelligent question to the effect that they might just get out of town and leave the geeks behind. Quinn answers that if the Dream Masters can invade dreams, running away won't do any good.

HOLD THE PHONE. They're still trying to decide if this power exists, and yet Quinn can state categorically the limitations of the power! Wouldn't a scientist wonder about the operating range of a Dream Master? Maybe getting out of town would work. Furthermore, this seems a perfect time to discuss how much time they have before the next slide. A human being can stay awake a long time if necessary, as I found out from doing this episode guide in record time.

Quinn and Rembrandt find the conveniently located Dream Masters club. More nerdy guys show up and argue with them about the merits of somnambulism, metaphysics, and whether or not Wade is a bitch. Do our heroes worry about being slapped with pentagrams? Nah. Everyone sort of threatens everyone and then the nerds go into the club.

The attentive viewer must be wondering why it is that all the bad guys are physically alike. It's as if our heroes have entered a world where all the bad guys are of the same race or the same religious or ethnic group.

Back in the hotel room, Arturo is asleep. At least that keeps him from suggesting that she sleep. Wade remains awake. She leaves a note and goes downstairs for a double espresso. Helping her to stay awake is Gerald, who hassles her in the bar. At no point does she try to pump the villain for any information even though he is obviously smitten with her. (She kept talking to the Kromaggs when she thought Quinn's life was at stake.) But with her own life threatened, she simply acts scared which is obviously what Gerald enjoys.

Gerald places his hand on her thigh. The pentagram appears and then fades. Does this mean that he hadn't touched her yet? (That was a bit unclear back at the pier.) In which case he couldn't invade her dreams, at least not very seriously if the death of the skater taught us anything. In which case she was perfectly safe so long as she stayed in the room, and she could have gone to sleep.

In the grand tradition of truly miserable writing, we may now assume that Wade will be sleeping very soon.

After Wade recovers from her first bout of dream-induced clichés, she suggests that there might be a hotel doctor who could give her some drugs to keep her awake.

We finally arrive at the dumbest moment. Arturo discourages the idea because (I'm quoting because I don't dare paraphrase here): "This planet's pharmacology might be harmful to your Earth Prime cell structure."

HOLD THE PHONE (AGAIN). I can't believe that a supposed science-fiction writer could make such a mistake. This is no ad lib. It's in the script. Look, the Sliders eat and drink in most of the worlds they visit. They have no choice. They didn't bring a lifetime supply of Earth Prime food and water. If they can handle the food and beverages of this silly Dream Master world, then why can't they handle drugs from the same world? Chemistry is chemistry.

Let's cut to the chase. Rembrandt is left to watch Wade. He drinks drugged coffee and falls asleep. She sleeps and suffers various out-takes from horror movies that we've all seen before. There's some tension between Arturo and Rembrandt when the prof accuses the other of dereliction of duty. Later, when Arturo finds out that Rembrandt was drugged, there is a painfully awkward apology scene that defies my poor powers of description.

Oops, I forgot about Wade. She's still trapped inside Nightmare on Sliders Street. But she survives. The Dream Masters are annoyed that she hasn't died of fright because once they mark someone for death it hurts their rep if the victim lives. The one older guy in their unique society, the man who made the discovery to empower nerds, orders Gerald to finish off Wade. Gerald's minions have faith in him. Obviously Gerald is next in line to become Head Nerd.

The room from which the Dream Masters send out their bad vibes has a most interesting feature. There's a girl dancing in there. A stripper? They never seem to notice her. She never seems to notice them. Maybe if they noticed her they could leave people's dreams alone. The implication is that if you give nerds the power of the gods, they still won't be able to get laid. Considering what anyone can do with a little money and a little power, this premise is utter nonsense.

The Sliders go to a secret medical facility where victims fight the bad guys. Despite Arturo's speech about the dangers of alternate earth pharmacology, the three male Sliders are put under so that they can find Wade in her dream and help her against the scary stuff.

The final confrontation is between Quinn and Gerald. Never mind that the confrontation needs to be between Wade and Gerald. The half-hearted feminism underlying the choice of villains collapses from the final insult that Wade can't even save herself. God, I hated that.

Anyway, the experienced Dream Master throws a fireball at Quinn. Quinn catches the fireball. Quinn does the one thing no master criminal would ever anticipate: throws the fireball back. Would an experienced practitioner of this hocus pocus be completely unprepared for a victim who fights back? Why, of course. Villains are never prepared for the least resistance.

POOF goes the Dream Master, inside the dream. Goodness and light have prevailed. The heroes slide in twelve hours. No way they could have used drugs for all of them to stay awake for a few days. Drugs are bad.

I don't want to end on a completely sour note, even for this episode. So here's a round of applause for a splendid single shot with Zack Ward. After his dream self is burned up by the fireball, we see the Dream Master exiting the conference room where he's been doing his dirty work. One of his arms is on fire and he pats it out. The actor did this fire gag himself. What a pro.

(PERSONAL NOTE: When I did the pitch for a carnival attraction for my movie producer friend Fred Olen Ray, I saw him do fire gags with Kim, the lovely lady who was to become his wife. Jeff Murray, his carnival partner, told me stories of how dangerous it is to do fire gags and I always remember that when I see anyone do one. So "The Dream Masters" has some entertainment value for me after all!)

DESERT STORM

Written by Matt Dearborn
Directed by Jim Johnston
Music by Stephen Graziano

GUEST STARS:

Gina Philips as Devin
Kristofer Lindquist as Jeremy
Ken Steadman as Cutter
Michael Lee Gogin as Master Healer
Lester Barrie as Diggs

WITH:

Constance Forslund as Fiona
Christopher Maleki as Wolf
Judson Mills as Davy
Gabriel Christy as Man
Chris Nash as "Cutter Double"

In the previous discussion of "The Dream Masters," I complimented Zack Ward for doing a fire gag. Many actors like to do their own stunts when feasible. In action films and television, it is a point of honor for performers to get in there and do some of the physical scenes.

This book is dedicated to the memory of Ken Steadman, who died during the production of "Desert Storm" in an accident with one of the dune buggies.

∞ ∞ ∞

Jerry O'Connell: "He was a terrific guy. One of these guys who always had a smile on his face. As an actor, he was willing to take any chances. He really had his craft down. I remember when I was working with him, I thought: 'Wow, this guy has really got it.' It was a shock and it was very sad."

Sabrina Lloyd: "We were in the makeup trailer and he just made me feel better than anybody about the show. He had such kind words for me. He was such a supportive person. He said, 'You guys have no idea how much you shine on camera. You should be really proud.' I thanked him. He really made me smile. He was a wonderful man."

Now a memory from someone not associated with *Sliders*, the screenwriter who wrote Ken Steadman's last movie, *Hindsight*.

Steve Tymon: "If there's one thing I really remember about Ken, it was the seriousness and intensity he brought to his craft as an actor. He had the drive that made him stand out from the crowd that said he was going to make it or else. To hear that he was finally regularly appearing on television (*Sliders, Bay Watch, NYPD Blue* and others) . . . to know that he'd begun making it, and then hear it end, was not only totally unexpected but completely unfair. It was one of the darkest moments of all my time in Hollywood."

∞ ∞ ∞

In this story, Earth has been seriously beaten up. The Pacific Ocean is gone, replaced by a vast stretch of stinkin' desert. H_2O is God to the surviving humans. Survival is a dicey proposition. The best way to sum it up is: Water catastrophe (pronounced 'Wotta Catastrophe'!).

We begin with the Sliders having a typical argument as they trek toward the remains of L.A. It becomes a meta-argument, arguing over having an argument.

At the Last Chance Cantina, they run into an old friend, the waiter Diggs, who has his best part in the series in "Desert Storm." (Note: in this season, he's been to waiting tables what Pavel is to driving cabs.) His first scene portrays something that I think would be a more frequent problem for Sliders than they normally encounter. How do they pay for stuff world to world? In this dried-up land, money is no good. You must barter.

Diggs offers them the bill of fare, which consists of two kinds of water: expensive clear and cheaper brown. Quinn offers his wristwatch in payment but Diggs turns it down because it runs on batteries and there's no way to replace those. He inquires if they have any tools or skins or gold. Nada. He won't even take Wade's necklace, and he's in no position to offer water for free. But he makes it as clear as his good water that he'll trade if they come up with anything he can use.

Wade is distraught at the ill treatment of a girl, Devin, who is brought, tied and gagged, into the cantina. First impressions can be deceiving, though. Devin is not a slave in any conventional sense. She has the power to find water, the power of life and death.

Wade hears Devin's cries for help . . . telepathically. The gag can't stop mental messages. The Sliders rescue her from her somewhat pathetic captor. Devin is grateful and promises that her powerful protector will reward them with lots of water. Devin is his water priestess.

Good old Diggs is a savvy merchant, and he's offering lots more than water for the right price. Such as a truck and lots of fuel. In payment, he takes gold from Jeremy (the man who was Devin's captor until the roles were reversed). To Devin's dismay, he insists she give up her amulet because he prizes its crystal. She reluctantly agrees.

Leaving the makeshift town behind, they encounter armed men

on motorcycles. Ken Steadman dominates his scenes as Cutter. "I'm not gonna kill you," he tells the Sliders when they bring Devin to him. "Consider the debt paid."

If there seems a slight discrepancy between Devin's promises of water and the actual deal, this is merely the fine print of a typical Hollywood negotiation. Cutter even offers to let the strangers follow along and have a drink on him, if they manage to keep up. (He's a saint next to El Sid.) It's the best offer they've had in a while. They live through a storm. They survive Cutter's hospitality. They witness Devin do her dowsing.

Wade asks Devin about her life as a water witch. In a cute bit, Wade refers to the storm as "big special effects." The two women begin to hit it off.

Later, Jeremy tries to kidnap Devin again but snatches Wade by mistake. He belongs to a different tribe. Cutter and his men go on a hunt for Wade and Jeremy. Their primary motive seems to be to take out Jeremy so he won't be trying to kidnap Devin anymore. The secondary motive is to put on war paint and rev their engines.

Jeremy and Wade survive their long trek through the desert. Quinn, Arturo, and Rembrandt find them before Cutter and company arrive. Wade complicates the situation by informing her friends that Jeremy is the good guy and Cutter, despite his winning ways and classy sartorial sense, is actually the bad guy. Jeremy has told Wade that Devin is a member of his tribe and that she doesn't know this because Cutter kidnapped her when she was five.

Cutter shows up and chases Jeremy. Quinn steps in and fights with Cutter. Quinn cuts Cutter. Our heroes escape with Devin, even though she doesn't seem the least bit interested in being rescued.

Cutter, bloodied and frustrated, resolves not to be a nice guy any longer.

On the trip to find the good tribe, Devin argues with Wade about the many virtues of Cutter. He's big. He's strong. Did she mention that he's big? Wade suggests that Devin trust the telepathic messages Devin starts picking up as they draw near the good tribe.

Arturo becomes sick.

Meanwhile, Cutter discovers Devin's amulet on Diggs and takes it. No trade. No haggling. He just takes it. Diggs is interested in keeping his teeth. Cutter believes the amulet proves there is a whole tribe of water people and he can use the amulet as a homing device to track down everybody.

The good tribe of democratic water people is found and Wade is vindicated completely. When Devin is reunited with her mother, she has a flashback to when Cutter killed her father. This makes up the mind of the water witch. She doesn't like Cutter anymore. (I still like him better than El Sid.)

Unaware that his water witch has switched sides, Cutter finds the location of the good tribe and suddenly realizes the quantity of water that must exist underground. Such a boon might even reduce the agony of losing Devin's love.

In a marvelous scene, Arturo goes to the master healer of the tribe, who is a total fraud (a swell performance by Michael Lee Gogin). For all the times the professor is subjected to hocus pocus that works, challenging his most basic assumptions about the scientific method, it's refreshing for Arturo to find a genuine faker, a glorious quack. Arturo is ill but he's not dying. He's getting better. The visit to the healer provides entertainment value, and the man does give Arturo a nice mint.

The climax is basic action material. Cutter and his men attack. The water people drop rocks on the invaders. Cutter grabs Rembrandt as a hostage, holding a knife on him. Devin uses her guile to trick Cutter into releasing Rembrandt; she then uses her powers to do serious damage to the poor man's brain. He falls to the ground, dazed, glassy-eyed. Gotta watch out for those water babes. At least she doesn't tell him that he needs to get on with his life.

The Sliders slide.

DRAGONSLIDE

Written by Tony Blake and Paul Jackson
Directed by David Livingston
Music by Danny Lux

GUEST STARS:
Michelle Rene Thomas as Melinda
Gregory Martin as Gareth
Francoise Robertson as Alesha
Max Grodenchik as Skuldar
Francis Guinan as Sean Nuinn
Lester Barrie as Diggs

WITH:
Charlie O'Connell as O'Hara
Saxon Trainor as Kelley
Mansell Rivers-Bland as Chief Druid
Sean Moynihan as Phillip Mallory

Let me say at the start that I'm fond of fantasy. When I was a wee lad, it was Ray Harryhausen's *The Seventh Voyage of Sinbad* that hooked me into strange stuff. So I became a writer instead of a corporate lawyer. I love dragons and wizards.

But if the Sliders enter a world of magic, I'd like a science-fiction explanation, such as the thoughtful one provided for "Into the Mystic." Science fiction should play fair, the same way mysteries do. Unfortunately, this episode is the first to give us hard-core fantasy. No explanations allowed.

The Sliders seemed more afraid in the world of "Into the Mystic" (where they find an explanation) than in "Dragonslide" (where they don't). I believe the reality would be just the opposite. This is a far more frightening world. The reason characters in fairy tales aren't catatonic or driven insane is because fantasy is the only world they know. The modern mind would crack if confronted by the following:

Once upon a time, there was a fair maid named Melinda who was apprenticed to a cruel Druid named Gareth. One day, she could no longer abide him and fled into the woods. Gareth sent an ugly gnome of a man named Skuldar to bring her back or suffer his displeasure. Skuldar caught the damsel.

Her prayers were answered when a magical blue tunnel opened in the air and brought into the woods four travelers: a big bear of a man, a tall youth, a dark-complexioned troubadour, and another lass as fair as Melinda. These wizardly travelers frightened Skuldar, who had magic of his own and transformed himself into a hawk that flew back to the castle of his brooding and unforgiving master.

Pity poor Skuldar who returned empty-clawed—er, empty-handed—and told his remarkable tale. He would have suffered mightily if not for recognizing that the tall youth was a Mallory. There must be some great secret of the Mallory clan on this world. Gareth hates anyone who is a Mallory.

How would the cruel Gareth like to find out that this young Mallory is smitten with his Melinda? The others will be his enemies as well. The big bear of a man is a sage named Maximillian. The troubadour is Rembrandt of the Many Tears, and the comely lass is Mistress Wade. These good comrades travel together and find markings of the Druids.

Alas, the police find them and they foolishly give over Melinda to their care. The police deliver her straight to Gareth, her lord and master. The policeman affirms that Gareth may do with the girl as he pleases. The policewoman has doubts but performs her duty anyway.

The wizardly four go to a tavern known as the Dragon's Breath Inn. Rembrandt of the Many Tears is smitten by a woman, Alesha by name, whose fair image he carries in his heart through all his journeys. But goblins have infested her heart in this world and turned her into a psychiatrist.

Maximillian and the troubadour quarrel about not having a sufficiency of damsels in their lives, all the while ignoring the comely lass who is at their side. Methinks they are all blind. Methinks Mistress Wade could see to the needs of all her traveling companions.

Other maidens have tougher rows to hoe. In the dark and cold castle of Gareth, poor Melinda suffers by the hour. Her master tells her that he waits for the right time to use his black art to raise a demon and make Melinda heavy with its child. The policewoman finds the maid and seeks to free her from her bonds but Gareth slays the cop.

Ere the policeperson dies, she must listen to Gareth tell of his plan, leaving out nothing. He's come up with a better idea than demonic impregnation. He will use Melinda as bait to draw young Mallory to the castle so that Gareth may possess his supposedly immortal body.

A vain and foolish man, the dark Druid does not know that young Mallory is a mortal—although a practitioner of an arcane form of magic known as science in the mysterious and far away land of block grants.

Melinda (out of the castle again) finds Mallory and implores that he spend some quality time with her. Wisdom in the head is no protection against folly lower down in the...heart. Beware, young Mallory, her siren call that fires the blood hotter than a dragon's breath.

Meanwhile, Mistress Wade is not idle but shows a talent for witchery by forming a magic circle on the floor using powder, and performing a love ritual so as to make Alesha of the shrunken heads fall under the spell of the troubadour's hungry eyes. Rembrandt falls in love with Mistress Wade instead.

Melinda kisses Mallory, rendering him stiff as a board. His whole body, I mean. The kiss was a bad idea: it immobilizes him, leaving him at Melinda's mercy.

She takes him back to Gareth's castle, apologizing that when her cruel master compels her to do something she is powerless to resist. In another world, the maid might consider a career as an actress. In this world, Gareth performs the ritual of transference, and his soul enters the body of what he believes to be the Wizard Quinn and a life of immortality.

Rembrandt is so smitten with Mistress Wade that he follows her everywhere until she turns to Alesha, who uses the magic of hypnosis and blather to break the spell. Then the troubadour expresses a safe, non-carnal love for Wade (poor guy).

Maximillian the Sage goes to the dark castle in search of Mallory and learns of the stealing of his friend's body. If Quinn Mallory is the mortal Maximillian says he is, then it's possible to exorcise Gareth's soul from the flesh. Disguised as a Druid, Maximillian enters a forest ceremony where he proves that the Mallory body is mortal by driving a blade into it. This forces Gareth to vacate the body and reclaim his own.

Melinda is able to heal Mallory only be releasing all her magic, including that which has kept her face beautiful. The maid sacrifices her physical beauty as deep scars appear, covering one side of her face.

Gareth is more cruel and vengeful than ever. He takes on the form of a fire-breathing dragon and seizes Melinda. They follow her with a new companion of their own, a falcon to chase away the hawk that Skuldar will become.

Vanity goeth before the fall of even a dragon. A sword forged by Merlin hangs on the dungeon wall of Gareth's castle. Only one of Mallory's clan can wield the mighty blade; he does and slays the venomous, scaled beast. The dragon turns back into a wounded Gareth.

This releases the last Mallory of this world, a charming prince of a fellow named Philip. He is reunited with his love, who is Melinda. Her face is beautiful to him—whatever lines cross its cheeks. When Gareth turns into a bug and tries to crawl away, Philip crushes it.

As the Sliders leave for new adventures, Philip and Melinda embrace, bringing the story to its only proper conclusion: And they lived happily ever after.

THE FIRE WITHIN

Written by Josef Anderson
Directed by Jefery Levy
Music by Stephen Graziano

GUEST STARS:
Anthony Tyler Quinn as J.C. Ashton
Brigitta Dau as Amanda
Lynn Clark as Diana Sylvius
Terry Markwell as TV Reporter
Ferdinand Carangelo as Foreman

WITH:
Veronica Cartwright as Flame (Voice-over)

Imagine a world where a cartoon flame creature chases after visiting humans so as to give them a hard time when they find jobs at an oil refinery. I'm not mad. I swear I'm telling the truth. Well, the flame creature is probably computer generated, so maybe it's unfair to call it a cartoon.

Are we still talking about *Sliders*? After last week's visit to Fairy-Tale Land, a flame creature is probably inevitable. If hard-headed Arturo could drive a blade into Quinn in the belief that the lad was possessed by an evil Druid and that another Druid would have the power to magically cure the mortal wound, then there is no one left to question anything.

On the other hand . . . a cartoon flame critter? A spunky little red-hot fire devil who just wants to be a pal?

The teaser is the best part. Rembrandt is batting in a simulated baseball game. He's placed a bet, using the Sliders' whole bankroll. Trouble is that they have to slide before he finishes the game, even though he was winning. Quinn should keep the Crying Man better informed on the time.

They find themselves in one of their classic good/bad situations. The bad news is that they're on an Earth that is burning up. The good news is that they'll only be there for ten seconds. They slide while they're still "rare." (What happens if they ever reach an Earth that's lost its atmosphere? Cancellation, probably.)

They reach a livable Earth just in time. Quinn's coat is on fire. He puts it out and dumps it in a trash can. Rembrandt says maybe they've just visited hell.

A small flame jumps out of the can and starts following the Sliders. Of all the places to bring an animated flame, they're in a company town run by Pan Global Oil. Since Rembrandt lost their money in the previous world, they'll have to get jobs here.

The plot: The fire-thing follows them around because it's an intelligent life form and realizes that its only hope of getting home is to stay near the entities who know how to slide. A bit of science fiction is included to the effect that the alien life form isn't really made out of fire but chooses fire as a resident energy source. Despite that insight, they could still give it a name. Scorchy would be nice.

Where the Sliders go, Scorchy goes. This is bad in an oil company town. Lots of gas around. Lots of oil. Hot air. Lots of stuff to burn. They get jobs at the oil refinery. Scorchy doesn't get a job, though. There's this scene in which Scorchy is riding on a truck, see, and the little critter has found a spot where it's sheltered from the wind.

'Course it leaves little flame tracks behind it. It has to burn to get places and that sets itty bitty fires. Each little piece of flame is still linked to the whole, another of those collective life forms that exist only in sci-fi.

So to hitch a ride on the truck, Scorchy ignites some grease on the axle so that it can climb up to where it can sort of sit, sheltered from the wind. I can't stand it. I can't go on.

Readers will certainly wonder why I chose "The Dream Masters" as the worst episode when there's this one. Once again, the answer is that "The Dream Masters" had potential. It could have been good.

But when it comes to The Sliders and Their Little Fire Pal, there's simply no way on God's green Earth to do anything with this idea. It would defeat Hemingway, Faulkner, Twain, Tolstoy, Shakespeare, Homer. Ed Wood would turn down the idea for one of his movies.

The Sliders are suspected of arson.

The Sliders are framed for arson.

The oil company is run by mean people who make the workers eat bad food and don't care much for unions. Finally, Scorchy can take no more and threatens to torch the town. There's plenty of methane gas and oil available to toast everyone in the vicinity.

Not to worry. Quinn communicates with Scorchy! First, Arturo notes that the flame creature divides like a cell. Capturing one flame is as good as capturing another when dealing with collective alien intelligence. Quinn traps a Scorchy in a container with liquid it can ignite and then covers the jar. They feed it oxygen to keep it alive. They also cut the oxygen off periodically to let it know that the humans are in control.

Never mind what a tremendous leap it is from recognizing a life form to assuming intelligence in said life form. What if Scorchy only had the intelligence of a dog? Then we could call it Sparky. Quinn and Arturo use a computer, a spectrometer, and a beaker to produce...the voice of Veronica Cartwright. Well, why not? Anything to speed the story to its pyrotechnic conclusion.

It's smooth sailing after that. Scorchy should no longer be thought of as an "it." She helps them stand off the bad guys. She even takes on a human shape. She trusts Quinn enough to join all her parts together, even though that would make it easier to destroy her. He sure knows how to talk to ladies who are really hot.

When they slide, they give Scorchy a ride on a box of matches, on which she burns the words: THANK YOU.

If there's any justice in this old universe, the next world they reach should be run by Smoky the Bear.

THE PRINCE OF SLIDES

Written by Eleah Horwitz
Directed by Richard Compton
Music by Danny Lux

GUEST STARS:
 Dan Gauthier as George Stellos
 Victoria Mahoney as Duchess Danielle
 Hallie Foote as Lady Mary
 Clinton Derricks-Carroll as Rembrandt #2

WITH:
 Terry Markwell as Anchorwoman
 Collin Bernsen as Captain of the Guards
 Tom Astor as Guard
 Gabrielle Beimforde as Nurse
 Kristopher Logan as Assassin
 Paul Goodman as Guard (A-15)
 Marian E. Green as Mother
 Brooke Elizabeth Crocker as Little Winged Girl Kahlee
 Elizabeth Barrio as Little Winged Girl

What a relief to return to a genuine alternate history again. This is a world in which America is a monarchy (descended from King Thomas Jefferson and his second wife, the former slave Sally Hemmings). In modern times, an epidemic has wiped out the female population's ability to gestate beyond the fifth month. A medical breakthrough allows for men to carry babies to term.

The Sliders don't know about the pregnancy situation right off the bat. They find that they enjoy many aspects of this monarchist America. They are amused to find out that in this world Rembrandt's double's wife (and the double herself of Rembrandt's lost love) is Duchess Danielle.

When the woman is rushed to the hospital about to lose her baby, and this world's Rembrandt is nowhere to be found, the Crying Man doesn't think twice about offering help. Too bad he didn't think once. He assumes they must want a blood transfusion. Danielle and he had the same blood type back home so the odds are they do here, as well.

This would all be well and good except the doctors don't want to do a blood transfusion. They want to transfer the baby from the duchess's body into Rembrandt's.

Quinn figures out what is going to happen to Rembrandt but is too late to stop the procedure. He enters the operating room and tries to tell his friend what to expect but Rembrandt has already been prepped and he's floating on Cloud 9. Quinn can't work out a way to get him past the nurse who gave him the sedative.

Remmy goes under a happy man, having found a world where he has his Danielle and the fans call him "Your Grace." He wakes up preggers.

While he was undergoing the operation, Arturo saved Quinn from being dragged off by convincing the authorities that he, Quinn, and Wade are the Duke's new personal assistants. The Lady Mary helps in this subterfuge because, apparently, she saw the Sliders together as friends before Rembrandt was asked to help in the medical emergency.

Thinking quickly, Arturo says that Wade is the Duke's nutritionist, Quinn is the fitness instructor, and Arturo is the man the Duke called in London and asked to assemble a team of professionals to help during the pregnancy.

They all end up in the royal mansion. Wade learns that although Rembrandt's double in this world could never be king because he's a commoner, the baby will be fourth in line for the throne. Arturo learns more about the medical technology and fills in the aptly named Crying Man on the process of shared pregnancy. The doctors implant an artificial womb to carry the baby. At first, Rembrandt is not as upset as might be expected for reasons any woman who's been pregnant can appreciate. He's too far gone, too sleepy, too . . . pregnant to be freaking out. Cleavant Derricks has a lot of fun with the role, especially when Crying Man finally understands his condition.

Rembrandt's love for Danielle is a factor to be considered as well. So long as she thinks he's her man, and he's carrying her baby, he makes the most of it. How many men would carry a baby for the woman they love? Eleah Horwitz must have had fun writing this.

Lady Mary turns out to be a baddie. Her hireling was supposed to have assassinated Rembrandt (this world's version), and he insists that he saw Rembrandt disappear in the ocean. She wants her illegitimate child to inherit the throne. She gives the failed assassin a bad report consisting of a literal knife in the back.

Shortly thereafter, the news reports that the king and his children have died in a mysterious accident. Rembrandt wonders what this means. Only that his baby is the king in utero! Time for Lady Mary to plot against the expectant Slider, who has just discovered another problem.

Danielle figures out that this Rembrandt is not her Rembrandt. What gave him away was his happy singing. Her Remmy was completely tone deaf. He levels with her and promises that her baby is safe with him. Fortunately, her first instinct is not to call the guards.

Quinn and Wade succeed in finding the real duke, adding some legitimacy to Lady Mary's reason for assassinating her assassin. Rembrandt #2 is thrilled that his son is going to be king, but he wants to know who's carrying him. They have the same problem with him that Rembrandt is having with Danielle. Sliding is not the easiest thing to explain.

Danielle solves a lot of the problems by believing enough of the incredible story. She realizes that the baby must be transferred from our Rembrandt to her Rembrandt. Lady Mary goes into high gear with one last scheme but she doesn't reckon on the rebellion of her illegitimate son, who did not know the truth about himself (he thought Lady Mary was his aunt) or what she was up to. He helps to thwart her nefarious scheme, the ungrateful fellow.

Lady Mary's son helps them find Arturo, Danielle, and the Rembrandts (sounds like a rock group). She orders the cabin in which they're staying set on fire. They all survive but the unborn king is in danger from all the smoke Rembrandt inhaled. Arturo has to deliver the baby from Rembrandt's artificial womb. Lady Mary's bastard proves his nobility by stopping her from killing anyone else. He personally places her under arrest.

This is a good episode, and what's best about it is that it provided Cleavant and his brother a chance to work together again. The Duke loves Danielle but he takes her for granted, the one thing our Rembrandt would never do. Before the slide, Rembrandt helps the Duke understand how fortunate he is to be married to this woman.

STATE OF THE ART

(the original script was titled STATE OF THE A.R.T.)

Teleplay by Nan Hagan
Story by Schuyler Kent
Directed by John Kretchmer
Music by Stephan Graziano

GUEST STARS:

Eddie Mills as Deric
Robert Englund as James Aldohn
Kathleen McClellan as Erica (Shauna)
Jerry Rector as Paul
Jeff Rector as Scarface Paul

WITH:

Ted Detwiler as T.E.D.

This is a fairly routine treatment of oh-my-god-the-actors-are-robots, but with some nice touches. There's the advantage of a guest appearance by Robert Englund, a character actor who is one of today's true horror stars.

The Sliders land in a world where the sky is the color of fresh lilacs. Although they are in the middle of a city with functional stop lights and streetlights, there is no one to be seen. Turning a corner, they come across the skeletal remains of a humanoid robot. The electronics have been cannibalized. The eyes are missing. (Hmmmm, mechanical Kromaggs, maybe?)

When they hear the roaring of an engine and running feet, they discount the abandoned city idea. We return to a more familiar situation, and the Sliders once again prove they could enter the Olympics and do the fifty-yard dash. Behind them comes a Humvee (left over from the pilot?) firing laser blasts. The others make it to the safety of an alley but Quinn is hit by the laser and engulfed in an electrical field that knocks him out. The runners being chased by the Humvee are also taken down.

One of the soldiers carries a meter that picks up something, but it can't be life signs. Although he is standing at the mouth of the alley, the Sliders fail to register on his device. The soldiers leave Quinn behind.

Quinn is not dead and he regains consciousness. He's not even sick, only tired. They check the timer. They only have to survive Sci-Fi World for three days. Then they examine one of the downed runners. The "man" is a robot.

Arturo realizes that the meter device must be attuned to the electronic signature of androids. The man on the ground has a little juice left and tries to tell them something. Quinn guesses which wires go where. Arturo helps by recognizing the similarity of android innards to human anatomy. By some miracle, they actually repair a highly sophisticated piece of technology they have seen for the first time.

The artificial man is called Deric, an acronym for the Delta model of the Emotional Response Intelligence Chip unit. He is fascinated to learn that his rescuers are human beings. Time for another crash course in a new world's history. Humans built robots. Robots took over. Film at eleven.

There are details. Aldohn Robotic Technologies built the robot work force to free mankind from the drudgery of having something to do. The man behind all this is still around, James Aldohn. He is now referred to as Father. Deric is programmed to feel emotions, which means he'll make a better companion than some characters who've crossed their paths.

The men in the Humvee are also robots, part of the RPU, the Re-call Patrol Unit. The members of the unit are called Pauls, and their main directive is to destroy the ERIs (Emotional Response Intelligence models), of which Deric is a prime example. The reason is that Father is "recalling" these units because they can self-program—a modern version of free will. Father is afraid of what he can't control, so marriage is definitely out for this guy.

Now that the situation has been explained, it's all right for the RPU to return and do a better job this time. The bad news is that they capture Quinn and Rembrandt. Vanessa the researcher notes that another of Quinn's shirts bites the dust. In fact, this time they have him down to his shorts. I should like to go on record right now complaining that Wade isn't captured and examined nearly enough.

Rembrandt and Quinn are introduced to Aldohn. The moment they see he is Robert Englund they should feel like they'd met Bela Lugosi, Boris Karloff, or Vincent Price. Mad scientists are always polite. They can afford to be. They also have the best dialogue. It's written into their contracts. He's delighted to have company. A new audience to lecture is a godsend.

Meanwhile, Wade believes that Deric can experience the full range of human emotions. Arturo has doubts. Wade kisses Deric. Deric kisses Wade. Deric may be a machine but he kisses Wade so well that she is disturbed by her own reactions. Just as the situation becomes interesting, Wade breaks it off. She has taught Deric the meaning of human loneliness.

At the robot factory, Father Aldohn gives Quinn and Rembrandt the full tour. While they watch robots being assembled, he tells how the robots revolted and exterminated the human race. According to him, the ERI's survival instinct is what destroyed Homo sapiens . . . with the exception of their creator.

He introduces them to a beautiful woman, Shauna. If this be cybernetics, let's make the most of it. She is modeled on his late wife. (Many a mad scientist is deeply romantic about a lost lover, in contrast to his more cynical view of mankind in general. The similarity of mad scientists to writers and artists is often noted.)

Aldohn invites his human guests to dinner. Quinn politely declines, suggesting that Rembrandt and he rejoin their companions on the outside. Shauna uses her considerable charms to persuade Quinn and Rembrandt to stay for a game of Monopoly.

When Quinn behaves as though the polite banter means something, Aldohn reluctantly drops the civility and his guards use force to retain them. He needs Rembrandt and Quinn. He's constructed two perfect replicas of them that have everything but eyes...and minds.

Turns out that the Pauls are modeled on Aldohn's son, who died when an automaton crushed him. It also turns out that Father never learned to build a perfect human brain. He's come up with the next best thing—he can take the human mind, the full personality and awareness, and then download this matrix into a mechanical substructure. He wants to try out this method on his guests.

Unaware of the dire peril confronting their friends, Arturo and Wade continue learning about this world from Deric. Arturo is able to perform a major boon for his host—a repair job on Erica, modeled on the same woman as Shauna (ably played by Kathlen McClellan). Despite the terrible state she was in, he has her up and running in a little over sixteen hours.

How is it that all of a sudden Arturo can perform miracles of mechanical dexterity? A good engineer will guess and trust his instincts, whereas a theoretical scientist will be stymied by his need to know WHY something works. Since "Gillian of the Spirits," Arturo has turned into a mechanical whiz.

Wade, Deric, Arturo, and Erica go into action. Erica's chip allows her to reenter the factory. She was among the first models Father recalled. Does that mean she has a chip on her shoulder?

Quinn and Rembrandt break out of their cell, thanks to an idea of Rembrandt's. Along with knowing how to conduct music, the Crying

Man is good at using everyday objects to conduct electricity (sorry) and short the electric lock on the door.

While Quinn and Rembrandt work at breaking out, Wade and Arturo work at breaking in. They come together. They thwart Aldohn's plans. But not before the obligatory laboratory scene in which Jerry O'Connell gets to play the Quinn robot with a sinister edge. Quinn is incapacitated on a table next to the robot as the mind transfer begins.

Rembrandt gets the drop on Aldohn with one of the lasers. Arturo removes a hand from a fallen Paul to extract a chip that will open the gates. After they leave, Aldohn reactivates the Paul who is still functional despite his missing hand. It's always a bad idea to leave a mad scientist alive and well in his lab.

In a final battle, a stray laser blast strikes Aldohn, revealing that he is...a robot himself! He enjoys a moment of total vindication before his artificial body gives up the ghost (mind). The experiment he intended to perform on Quinn was already a success on himself. Paul downloaded him. Aldohn's mind forgot how to walk (lost the motor skills)—hence the wheelchair. He also lost the living man's sense of morality.

Father's second demise allows John Rhys-Davies to ad-lib a horrendous pun: "Aldohn, all done."

The other best line I'll quote in full is what Wade says to Deric before she slides: "I'll think of you whenever the particles in the atmosphere catch the light waves and scatter them." Exactly what my ex-wife said to me.

SEASON'S GREEDINGS

Written by Eleah Howwitz
Directed by Richard Compton
Music by Danny Lux

GUEST STARS:

Chase Masterson as Kelly Welles
Allen Williams as Don Welles
Neil Roberts as Mr. Ted Bernsen
Jacqueline Obradors as Carol
Stuart Fratkin as Instructor

WITH:

Jody Curtis as Ginny
Paul Messinger as Priest
Sean Flynn Amir as Jason
Nikolaus Keelaghan as Kid #2

The Sliders are in the mood for holiday cheer after a visit to Pygmie World. They arrive on the Earth of the main storyline with bamboo-woven shields and a criticism of Wade for being too nice to a native boy. Seems the boy thought Wade would be agreeable about having his children. Unpleasantness ensued.

Their arrival in the new world disturbs a live sheep and donkey in a Nativity scene. Must be that time of year. No reason to expect anything bizarre or out of the ordinary about Christmas. Except for the giant mall hanging in the sky, of course.

No alternate history could possibly explain this episode, so why bother? Mall World simply is. Moved by the spirit of the season, the Sliders go to church to pray. Suddenly a woman comes out of nowhere and dumps her baby on Arturo.

With a little sleuthing (foreshadowing next week's episode), they learn the woman works at the mall, referred to by friends and foes alike as Sky-High Plaza. So it came to pass that the Sliders did ascend into the Heavens and did sit on the right hand of... Bernsen, the mall manager.

After leaving the baby with the priest, they reach the mall via a super-escalator. Not only is it two days before the slide, but it's also two days before Christmas. With the buying rush on, the Sliders pick up jobs easily: Arturo is Santa. Wade and Rembrandt are elves, complete with pointy plastic ears. Quinn gets to be a corporate guy in a tie.

They begin figuring out the system. There are instant credit loans available, all part of a debt-driven economy in which the store is the ultimate company town.

When Wade recognizes alternate versions of her father and sister, Kelly, she avoids them and laments that she'll probably never celebrate Christmas with her real family again. Maybe she senses the stress between this world's version of Mr. Welles and his daughter. He doesn't approve of her management job with the mall. For example, she docks a worker three weeks pay for spending too much money on her sick mother instead of making other purchases. And here I thought consumption was consumption, regardless of product.

Back on the job front, the most entertaining moments take place between Arturo Claus and the kiddies. When Santa tries convincing a boy to go with a chemistry set instead of a Sammy Spender Doll and gooey-ooze (hmmm, part of a chemistry set?), the kid explains the facts of life to the man in the red suit. Not even Santa can take the "X" out of Xmas.

Arturo finds the mother of the baby but she refuses to take back the child. Her reason is the incredible debt burden she's carrying. Better the child should be an orphan down on Earth, in the flats.

Wade's dad is gently persuasive, and she agrees to come home with him and let him prepare a meal for her. In his home, she learns that her double in this world died along with her mother in childbirth. Wade reminds Mr. Welles of her mother.

A new problem is that Rembrandt starts being sucked into the commercial mania. The TV ads. The jingles. Subliminals are part of the effectiveness of the media blitzkrieg. Remmy develops a compulsion to buy. He fills up their room with presents and almost picks

a fight with Quinn when his friend tries to break through the mental fog.

Arturo tracks down Carol again. (That's her name, honest.) You can run from Santa but you can't hide. She tells him everything. She used her last available credit to smuggle her baby down to the flats. She has a fantasy that she will be able to pay off the debt and then reclaim her son. What she suggests is impossible under the Mall System. He offers to help recover the baby some other way.

Carol is given a crash course in Reality: All the credit originates from an outfit called Crescent Vista Funding, which is tied directly to Bernsen in a scheme to hold the workers in permanent bondage with inflated interest. Rembrandt has a crash course too, and learns how he's been brainwashed through subliminals coming across the flickering TV screen.

So are the chains of bondage struck from the bodies of the exploited masses while consciousness is raised against the managerial class and its economic hooliganism. Standard Christmas message.

Mr. Welles confronts Kelly about her being part of such a corrupt system. Wade and Carol break into Bernsen's office to dig up the dirt on him. Bernsen isn't in his office because he's berating Arturo for being an out-of-control Santa. Too late! A whole bunch of kids would rather listen to Santa tell stories than receive free video games from the corporate boss. Arturo is a very good storyteller.

At Bernsen's office, Wade trips a security alert on the computer as Kelly discovers them. In sixty seconds, security will be alerted unless Kelly shuts it off. Kelly is not about to help until Wade proves they're related by telling her things about herself that only she could know. Even the small differences between Wade's Kelly and this Kelly are convincing for all their areas of similarity. Blood wins out over corporate loyalty and Kelly shuts off the security system.

Everything is Happy Holidays after that. Kelly defies Bernsen. Funny how what seemed to be an iniquitous system has been reduced to one guy's personal criminality. In the spirit of the season, Quinn convinces Bernsen to turn the other cheek. He achieves this by slugging the guy. Mommy gets baby back. The gateway opens just in time to be the most spectacular Christmas decoration the Welles family has ever seen.

This episode also includes a Christmas present for males in the audience: we are treated to a fine view of Sabrina Lloyd's navel.

MURDER MOST FOUL

Written by David Peckinpah
Directed by Jeff Woolnough
Music by Stephen Graziano

GUEST STARS:
Brian McNamara as Inspector Reed
David Purdham as Dr. Bolivar
Brigid Brannagh as Erin
Adam Wylie as Trevor
Suzanne Mara as Dr. Punch
Lester Barrie as Diggs

WITH:
Frank Castrina as Wonk
Holly Claman as Anne
Taylor Leigh as Mrs. Taylor
Carmen Nogales as Young Woman
Derik Van Derbeken as Security Man
Brandon Michael as Boy

The purpose of this particular episode seems to be dressing up John Rhys-Davies as Sherlock Holmes, even though he's given the assumed name of Reginald Doyle. But how do you possibly arrange for the Sliders to reach Victorian London and provide Arturo with the requisite accouterments? By sheer trickery, of course, and a script by executive producer Peckinpah.

The story does not begin well for Professor Arturo when he skids into a row of garbage cans that the others miss. Arturo is already pissed off in a world where only one thing will land you in more trouble than a bad attitude—and that's the wrong wardrobe in the wrong place.

While the others fail to get adequate service at this world's version of the Last Chance Bar, Arturo attempts to have the aroma of garbage removed from his attire. When someone bumps into him on the street and spills coffee on him, he doesn't act happy. His anger attracts authority figures. They are mental-health professionals of some kind. One jabs him with an awfully large needle. He is promptly dragged off to receive care.

Back at the bar, the Sliders begin to learn a few details about this current world. For example, they find out that casual clothes on the street would result in their being arrested the same as Arturo.

They dress yuppie style and head for the Evaluation Center. Before they even arrive, Arturo has already been sucked into the main plotline.

The docs think the prof is a fractal, the polite term for psychotic cases. They also believe Arturo to be a man of some quality, deserving of the very best treatment. Dr. Bolivar hypnotizes him and provides him with an alter ego. Permissive therapy, anyone? The way this works is that they take a crazy person and temporarily submerge his identity under an imaginary personality that speaks to something fundamental in the patient. Arturo is an aficionado of Sherlock Holmes. He becomes his own version, Reginald Doyle.

For some peculiar reason, the conditioning doesn't take without regular reinforcement from a pocket watch that glows every now and then and keeps Arturo dotty. Having learned of Arturo's problem, we promptly plummet into . . .

The Park. For the next few weeks, it will be a perfect recreation of Victorian London. A cast of supporting roles and extras will all play-act to help one guy try to overcome his psychological problems. Yeah, sure.

A number of important Scotland Yard positions are taken by the medical staff running this affair, but the general public is allowed to audition. Final cast includes Wade as a tart, Rembrandt as a bobby, and Quinn as Doyle's assistant.

Doyle's problem is to solve the Jack the Ripper murders. The first Ripper murder is staged. Apparently, only Arturo is expected to believe it. After he exits, the "murdered" girl returns to the land of the living. The minute Wade's new friend, Erin, expresses joy at receiving a note informing her that she is a D.V. (Designated Victim), everyone I saw the episode with screamed out, "Victim!!!" Like, we had a psychic flash, you know.

The best thing that can be said about the murder of Erin is that it gives Doyle a real murder to solve. Of course, he can't tell the difference between the simulated and genuine corpses so far. But as he begins comparing the unreal and the real, he begins overcoming the brainwashing.

Although Quinn has figured out that the pocket watch has something to do with keeping Arturo in his fantasy, he's been unable to get his hands on it. He should take lessons from the kid who steals the timer. (Quinn does retrieve it.) The kid provides the only real assistance in finding the murderer. Quinn even invites him to slide, but the kid passes.

Arturo confronts Bolivar in his rooms and proves to the doc that he is the killer. All Bolivar needs to do is put Arturo under again. There is only one possible explanation for the doc's penchant for mayhem. He's a . . . fractal! A real one. That's why he accuses innocent people of being fractals. In the best-directed scenes, the mad therapist attempts to carve up Wade, who puts up a hell of a fight.

She is wearing a most fetching red lady-of-easy-virtue dress. The Ripper must think her blood would go with the color of her outfit. She does not agree and succeeds in knocking him down in Arturo/Doyle's rooms. Instead of taking the opportunity to render him unconscious or deceased, she runs out into the street where he chases her.

The second time he tries to kill her, she gets away again. The third try looks as if Wade might be taking her last slide, but the other heroes finally show up and Rembrandt finally acts like a cop...I mean, bobby.

Even then, the mad doc tries to have everyone else arrested but there's too much evidence for him to talk his way out of it. No one even asks if he'll help bring Arturo out of his state of mental confusion.

The only thing wrong with this episode is that it doesn't make a lick of sense. The mad doc is a killer because he's crazy. He must be crazy to go to all this trouble to catch himself through his own patient's fantasy therapy.

The production values are terrific, however.

There are isolated scenes of John Rhys-Davies as the Victorian sleuth that are good all by themselves. He slides, still thinking he's Reginald Doyle.

NOTE TO THE READER:

"**M**urder Most Foul" was the last episode I saw before having to complete this book. An interesting coincidence is that it was the episode being filmed the day I did the interviews.

The remaining episodes will be summarized without critical commentary or story detail. They are single-paragraph summaries included for completeness.

However, I wouldn't want to stop at this point without expressing a thought about the big *Sliders* controversy. I am sorry that John Rhys-Davies is no longer with the show. He is a true gentleman and a major talent. At the time of the interviews, neither of us knew that he would be off the show by the time this book appeared.

The episode in which his character dies will be talked about for a long time.

Finally, a lot of fans are dumping on Kari Wuhrer. Hey, it's not her fault! So, stop it! But I'd like to blame someone for the loss of Sabrina Lloyd . . .

∞ ∞ ∞

SLIDE LIKE AN EGYPTIAN

Written by Scott Smith Miller
Directed by Adam Nimoy
Music by Danny Lux

GUEST STARS:

Apollonia as Dr. Deera Mubaric
Rocco Vienhage as Dr. Achtbit
Shaun Toub as Kheri-Heb
Claudette Mink as Sheilah
Armando Valdes-Kennedy as Seyn Jebid
Steven Meek as RDI agent

WITH:

Justin Gorence as Priest
Terry Markwell as Reporter

On an Earth where Egypt is still the politically and culturally dominant force, the Sliders disrupt an ancient burial rite that has spawned some scientific horrors. The first disruption occurs when Quinn rescues a beautiful young slave girl, and this leads to his apparent death. Later, inside a giant pyramid, it looks certain that the Sliders will slide without him, but the timer fails and its flashing lights enrage a biochemically engineered, giant mutated scarab. The insect's subsequent rampage causes the Sliders to be entombed inside the pyramid with the man-eating insect and an evil

Egyptian official. Out in the city, Quinn returns from the Land of the Dead, and now must find a way to reunite with the other Sliders, who are sealed in the pyramid.

PARADISE LOST

Written by Steven Stoliar
Directed by Jim Johnston
Music by Stephen Graziano

GUEST STARS:
Rob Youngblood as Sheriff Burke
Lara Steinick as Laurie Miller
Pat Stewart as Trudy Whitmore
Will Schaub as Parker
Kristi McDaniel as Alice

WITH:
Todd Babcock as Michael Levy
Jeff Markey as Bud
Gordon Jennison as Fred

The Sliders arrive face first in the sand in a small town called "Paradise," a place frozen in time. They notice very few people on the street, and those they see are all under thirty years of age. While surveying the town, the Sliders encounter Laurie, a geologist. Upon learning that Laurie's assistant is missing, the Sliders decide to help her locate him. When asked about the missing assistant, everyone in the town clams up. Soon the Sliders discover a beast that lives beneath the ground. The townspeople have been keeping it alive with human sacrifice. The beast emits a blue goo that, when eaten, allows the people to look young until they die. Rembrandt and Quinn find the creature's cave and douse the beast's blue egg hatchery with gasoline. There is a grand explosion and everything goes up in smoke, including the beast. The nightmare is over and the Sliders escape.

THE LAST OF EDEN

Written by Josef Anderson
Directed by Allan Eastman
Music by Danny Lux

GUEST STARS:

Ron Melendez as Brock
Don Jeffcoat as Keegan

The Sliders find themselves in a beautiful forest on an alternate Earth during an unusual planetary alignment. Off in a meadow they see a dozen or more men, women, and children, none of whom appear to be more than eighteen years of age. Suddenly there is a low rumble, and the ground starts to vibrate violently. There is a mighty roar and the ground opens, causing a young woman and her baby to fall into the chasm below. The deep fissure

rips across the earth, heading directly towards Wade, who falls into the chasm. The inhabitants do not move to help because the Ja- neers, mythical creatures who live under the ground, forbid these people to leave this place and any death is considered a human sac- rifice that ensures good fortune. Below the surface of the earth, Wade finds an abandoned underground city. She follows the cries of the infant and discovers a female creature nursing the baby as if it were her own. Quinn and Wade rescue the baby and return to the surface. Because Quinn and Wade are able to return from below, the people who felt they could not leave this land for fear of the wrath of the Janeers start off on a journey to find a safe new land.

THE EXODUS
Part One

Teleplay by Tony Blake & Paul Jackson
Story by John Rhys-Davies
Directed by Jim Charleston
Music by Stephen Graziano

GUEST STARS:

Kari Wuhrer as Captain Maggie Beckett
Mark Kiely as Dr. Steven Jensen
Wes Charles Jr. as Malcolm
Linda Henning as Mrs. Mallory
Steve Larson as Street Person

SPECIAL GUEST STAR:

Roger Daltry as Colonel Rickman

WITH:

J. Karen Thomas as Lt. Teri Eastman
Krzystof Pieczynski as Dr. Jariabek
Michael Houston King as Dr. Baker

The Sliders land on an apocalyptic world threatened by intense radiation. Our Sliders are trapped since their timer will not allow them to slide to safety before the anticipated doomsday arrives. It is on this planet that we first meet Captain Maggie, whose husband has been successful with creating equipment to access parallel worlds. Maggie and Quinn are thrown together in an effort to save themselves. Meanwhile, a maniacal Colonel Rickman secretly aspirates brainstem fluid from unsuspecting victims and leaves them unconscious in an attempt to keep himself alive. As Part One draws to a close, it appears that Quinn and Maggie, in their search for a compatible earth, may have stumbled upon the Sliders' true "Home Earth." Unfortunately, they discover Maggie is unable to breathe on the Sliders' Earth. The Sliders are forced to abandon what may be Earth Prime to save Maggie's life by returning with her to her native Earth.

THE EXODUS
Part Two

Written by Josef Anderson & Paul Jackson and Tony Blake
Directed by Jefery Levy
Music by Danny Lux

GUEST STARS:
Kari Wuhrer as Captain Maggie Beckett
Mark Kiely as Dr. Steven Jensen
Wes Charles Jr. as Malcolm
Linda Henning as Mrs. Mallory

SPECIAL GUEST STAR:
Roger Daltry as Colonel Rickman

WITH:

Andrew A. Rolfes as Sergeant
Sandy Laufer-Blake as Nurse
Lisa Galiana as Woman
Reba Shaw Alexander as Secretary
Michael Houston King as Dr. Baker

Quinn and Maggie return to her home Earth. The Sliders take off again to find an Earth that can support human life. Unfortunately, by the time Arturo discovers Rickman's horrid secret, Rickman has already opened an evacuation vortex. When Rickman begins to shoot at the Sliders, Arturo sacrifices his own life to save his friends by taking the bullets. The Sliders pay a tearful farewell to their fallen comrade. Although deeply shaken by the loss of Arturo, Maggie, Quinn, Rembrandt, and Wade must use the timer's new tracking device to slide off in pursuit of justice for their friend.

SOLE SURVIVORS

Written by Steven Kriozere
Directed by David Peckinpah
Music by Stephen Graziano

GUEST STARS:

Stephanie Niznik as Debra Carbol
Jay Acovone as Dr. Tassler

Maggie, Quinn, Rembrandt, and Wade slide into a new world and find themselves tripping over the carnage of human remains. The Sliders discover the people of this Earth have been infected by a virus brought on by the use of a drug containing a bacteria engineered to attack fat. Along with an antidote, it was marketed as a diet drug. Unfortunately, the antidote was ineffective, and it quickly unleashed a population of frenzied, fat-seeking cannibals. When Quinn gets infected after being bitten, he fears he will go mad and eventually turn against his friends. Quinn asks Maggie to end his life to spare him the madness of such a fate. Maggie agrees to Quinn's request, but fortunately the Sliders are able to discover an effective antidote to the bacteria by using the blood of a young woman who has a natural immunity to the fat-seeking disease.

THE OTHER SLIDE OF DARKNESS

Written by Nan Hagan & Scott Smith Miller
Directed by Jeff Woolnough
Music by Stephen Graziano

GUEST STARS:
Oona Hart as Adra
Kevin Quigley as Bunt La Croix
Franc Ross as Billy T.

Kari Wuhrer as Maggie Beckett
Neil Dickson as Colonel Rickman

WITH:

Gregory Norman Cruz as Dagan
Amy Wheaton as Lucy La Croix

The Sliders arrive in a forest shrouded in thick yellow fog. After a quick check of the timer's vortex-tracking system, they confirm Rickman has also landed here and has yet to slide out. The Sliders meet up with Adra, an exotic, blind, tarot-reading "seer." She tries to warn them that they are in grave danger if they venture back into the forest. Quinn and Maggie set off into the forest after Rickman. Quinn encoutners Quinn #2, who explains that he has become a tortured shell due to his years of sliding alone. Quinn #2 made a deal with Rickman to lure Quinn to this Earth because he wants Quinn to kill him. Quinn refuses, and a fight between the two Quinns ensues. Just as the altercation turns deadly, Rembrandt and Wade arrive and create a diversion with Adra's bag of tricks. The Sliders are freed from the forest and slide to the relative safety of a new world.

THE BREEDER

Written by Eleah Horwitz
Directed by Paris Barclay
Music by Danny Lux

GUEST STARS:
Dawnn Lewis as Dr. Sylvius
Chip Mayer as Man
Lester Barrie as Elstin Diggs
Deborah Kellner as Tami
Spencer Garbett as Roger

WITH:
David Chisum as Paramedic
Alton Butler as Orderly
R. Todd Torok as D. Squad Captain
Paris Barclay as Bureaucrat

The Sliders arrive knee deep in murky water fighting off icky swamp critters. Although they slide off this earth in ten seconds, Maggie is accosted by a gelatinous, crab-like creature that attaches itself to her face and manages to invade her body when she opens her mouth to scream. When the vortex opens and they slide onto the next Earth, they discover Maggie lying motionless, green foam oozing from her mouth. The other Sliders discover the symbiont that invaded Maggie's body did so in an effort to breed. It uses Maggie as a seductress in an attempt to locate viable male subjects with which to procreate. With little regard for human life, Maggie sets off on a destructive rampage to secure males. With the help of a Dr. Sylvius, the Sliders successfully lower Maggie's body temperature to a point at which the symbiont is unable to comfortably exist within her. Quinn lures the symbiont out of Maggie's body, and Maggie is no longer under the symbiont's control.

SLITHER

Written by Tony Blake & Paul Jackson
Directed by Jim Johnston
Music by Stephen Graziano

GUEST STARS:

Julie St. Claire as Kyra
Randy Vasquez as Carlos
Marc Tissot as Don
Danny Mora as Angel
Thomas G. Waites as Randy
David Correia as Customs Official

In this world, Rembrandt and Quinn are bumped from their scheduled flight back to San Francisco to meet up with Wade and Maggie. They manage to maneuver a ride on a charter flight with a woman named Kyra who is transporting two rare snakes. When Wade and Maggie learn Quinn and Rembrandt's plane went down somewhere near a town called Delgado, they take off to find them. Meanwhile, Quinn, Rembrandt, and Kyra start off on foot, carrying the rather large female triadder snake in a trunk. The male triadder managed to slither out of the plane and into the fields and is presumed lost. Suddenly they find themselves besieged by hundreds of frenzied attack snakes led by the male triadder, who seeks to free his mate. The Sliders gain control of the situation by freeing the female snake, who takes off with her mate. Finally, left in peace, the Sliders open a new wormhole and slide out.

DINOSLIDE

Written by David Peckinpah
Directed by Richard Compton
Music by Danny Lux

GUEST STARS:
Rainer Grant as Gretchen
Neil Dickson as Colonel Rickman
Wes Charles Jr. as Malcolm
Michael Woolson as Andrews
Mike Terner as Hinds

WITH:
Robyn Lees as Woman

Rickman's appetite for brain fluid has increased to a fatal level forcing the Sliders to follow him with an increased sense of urgency. The Sliders hope the vortex they have jumped into will put an end to Rickman's reign of terror. When the vortex spits them out, they find they have gone backwards through the inner dimension and returned to the "New World" chosen for the survivors of Maggie's world in "Exodus." Unfortunately, the Sliders soon discover Rickman isn't the only creature whose appetite has increased. The Sliders find themselves in a deadly game of cat-and-mouse as they attempt to capture Rickman while being pursued by a hungry T-Rex. Ultimately they outsmart the mighty T-Rex but not Rickman, who manages to elude capture yet again.

STOKER

Written by Josef Anderson
Directed by Jerry O'Connell

GUEST STARS:

Ryan Alosio as Morgan
Neil Dickson as Colonel Rickman
Duff McKagan as Harker
Danny Masterson as Renfield
Tommy Chong as Van Elsinger

WITH:

Ted Rooney as Technician
Leslie Monique Soule as Mina
Barry Livingston as Eddie Selk
Lauri Pressler as Nurse
Anthony David as Security Guard

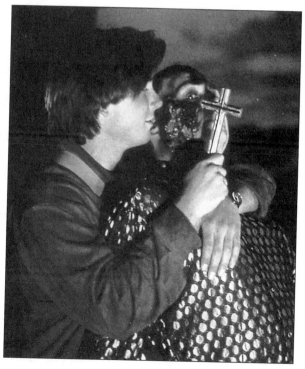

The Sliders continue their pursuit of the evil Rickman. When they arrive on a new Earth, the team splits up. Wade checks out a hot gothic rock band called "Stoker," at whose concert several alleged Rickman victims had last been seen. Wade's attempts to infiltrate the band and gain information on the Rickman connection brings her into the intoxicating charms of the lead singer, Morgan. Meanwhile, Quinn has teamed up with a man who's been trying to prove that Morgan and the rest of the band are vampires. Working together, they are able to rescue Wade before Morgan turns her into one of them. Unfortunately, Rickman once again manages to elude the Sliders, and they continue their pursuit of him in the next world.

THIS SLIDE OF PARADISE

Written by Nan Hagan
Directed by Jim Johnston
Music by Stephen Graziano

GUEST STARS:
Melinda Clarke as Alisandra
Neil Dickson as Col. Rickman
Deron Michael McBee as Ceres
Marc Riffon as Daniel
Michael York as Dr. Vargas

WITH:
Sam Gifaldi as Michael

The Sliders arrive on an island, in a lush jungle setting. In this world, the "Big One" finally may have hit, turning California into a series of small islands. The Sliders learn that Rickman is here and has managed to form an unhealthy alliance with Dr. Vargas, the leader of a tribe of "huminals"—half-human, half-animal hybrids that inhabit the jungle. Quinn, Maggie, and Wade are captured and Rembrandt finds himself caught between his utter repulsion for the doctor and his desperate need for the doctor's help in freeing the other Sliders. The Sliders are indeed freed and narrowly escape a marauding band of frenzied huminals. As they prepare to slide back to Earth Prime, Quinn and Maggie are attacked by Rickman and become separated from the other Sliders. Once rid of Rickman, Quinn and Maggie leap into a vortex. When the vortex reopens, they realize they are not on Earth Prime. Their damaged timer has slid them randomly into another world—a world from which they cannot escape.

END OF THIRD SEASON

PART SIX:
THE INTERVIEWS

Every fan has his or her favorite Slider. I've solved the problem of organizing this material by the simple expedient of running the interviews in the order I conducted them.

INTERVIEW WITH
CLEAVANT DERRICKS

BL: Cleavant, with your Broadway background, do you find anything theatrical about working on Sliders?

CD: There was one particular show that I did—I think three shows back—where it lent itself to the theater. It was a scene where Sabrina's character, Wade, gives me a potion for a girl that I'm interested in and the potion backfires so I fall in love with Wade. ["Dragonslide."] We temporarily have a whimsical kind of relationship. I had to express my love and my affection for Wade, and that lent itself to more of a theatrical aspect.

BL: What about "The King Is Back"? Seems like the ultimate Elvis-type fantasy, wasn't it?

CD: Yeah. That was one of my big shows. I think we did that the first season out. Because I'm a singer, I was able to have a lot of fun with that show. It presented real theater in the fact that I had to choreograph a lot of the moves. My brother came and joined me in that particular project. I have a twin brother, identical twin. They were able to do a lot of things with the camera that you would think, "Wait a minute! How did they do that?"

BL: You both work together in "Greatfellas" and "The Prince of Slides." I was thinking "God, those special effects are something!" That'll teach me to read the credits. Here I'm thinking Sliders *has the best optical work on TV.*

CD: Yep, so that's the secret behind that one! They do it with twins.

BL: I know "Greatfellas" meant a lot to Tracy Tormé, putting his father in it.

CD: We had a lot of fun working with Mel. He has a wonderful sense of timing and a wonderful sense of humor. There was one scene that I was able to work with Mel on. That was a scene where we were coming into the world and we had crashed a wedding. I look at Mel and I'm like, "Oh Mel Tormé! Lord, man, I love you! Remember when we did..." and he's looking at me like, "Guy, I don't know you. What are you doing?"—and his face was so hysterical it took me about six takes to do that because every time I would look at him, I would break up in laughter because he has this great sense of humor and this great expression on his face. I liked working with him. I'd heard he was in the hospital. I'm glad to hear that he's home and he's doing better.

BL: Who's idea was it to make him a country and western singer?

CD: His son's. Tracy has great wit and I like a lot of the shows that he sets up with us. He hasn't done much with the shows this season, this time around. I think maybe he's done one.

BL: Yeah, "The Guardian," but it's one of the best.

CD: It is Tracy Tormé. I mean, all of the characters, each one of the characters. Writing really counts.

BL: When I was doing the novel based on the pilot, I thought your character grew throughout the series, and I got permission to take some of the later things about your character and put it in the novel.

CD: Interesting. When I first read the script, I turned it down. I felt the character was written a little over the top, so he became more of a caricature than a character. I had a talk with Tracy about it and he promised that he would work this guy around to where he'd be a real human being. They've always had a prob-

lem with a character like this. Any time you take a character out of a pilot and you create this guy specifically for the human element, and the humor that's there, once you finish the pilot and they say, "OK, now we've got shows to do," you go back and you look at this guy again. Then you go, "Wait a minute, now what do we do with him?"

We needed him to get us started, but now that we've got him here, do we keep him, do we let him go? What do we do with him now? What kind of a background, really, does he have? How can he contribute? My suggestion was that, as long as you have Rembrandt, you should have him asking the questions that the audience would ask.

I said that as long as you keep him growing as he's asking questions, then you'll be able to find ways to develop this guy. Because, if he's asking questions, he's learning, as any student in a classroom would learn. Then we'll get a well-rounded character.

BL: *I thought about things like that for the novel. Remember the scene where he's suddenly transported to the other world and he runs into the iceberg? I figured if he'd been going too fast he would have killed himself when he's suddenly on an icy road.*

CD: Exactly. You know it.

BL: *Well, in the novel, I have Rembrandt deliberately slow down in the residential neighborhood in case there's a kid playing, and that's why he's not killed when he's pulled into the other world and is suddenly on the icy road! I did a whole bunch of little bits like that.*

CD: Yeah. I like that a lot. It's like you were looking at the situation and saying, "You know what, let's make it good, let's do it right."

BL: Even though he's got a lot of ego, he pays attention to other people and sometimes he can see things about other people that the scientists Quinn and Arturo might miss.

CD: That's right.

BL: Normal people things.

CD: Exactly, and I like that. I think we're doing a lot this season. I think we did some of it last season. Some people mentioned that Rembrandt was quite dark last season, no pun intended. I got a letter from one young man who said, "I really liked the way Rembrandt was in the first season. In the second season, they wrote him a little dark, a little angry. He was like the angry black man." I said we were looking for other avenues for stretching this guy, trying to find ways of broadening his character because we had done that in the first run of the show.

I liked the fact that he could stand up for himself. I liked the fact that he could be threatening and take care of business. There was one particular show that I liked where we went to the world where Quinn had befriended the little kid that was in the Western world. ("The Good, the Bad and the Wealthy")

BL: Yeah. I got a bunch of my lawyer friends together to watch that one with me. We all loved it.

CD: (Laughs.) There was a moment where Quinn seemed to shoot a guy and kill him. The Professor, Rembrandt, and Quinn were in the hotel room and Quinn was upset about this guy losing his life. Arturo was being sympathetic to Quinn and I deliberately played Rembrandt as being a little cold in a sense of: Look, the cards were dealt to you, you had to do it.

I liked playing him that way, because it was giving Rembrandt something else and stretches the character—which is what I was looking for at the time.

BL: Do all of you get along as well in real life as comes across on the tube?

CD: Yeah, it's a good group. The challenge is trying to make each character, who is coming from completely different backgrounds, contribute to a situation. But I find that fascinating because you can't put all of us in one basket. We play strong individuals. I think that's a feather in Tracy's cap. I love the fact that he went and brought in an R&B singer and put him in this predicament.

BL: It helps make it a smart show.

CD: It makes it challenging, for writers as well as the actors.

BL: So much of TV is boring. What's great about this show is that it reinvents itself every week.

CD: What we're looking for is to enlighten you and at the same time entertain you. Kids are falling into it. And I gotta tell you, I'm running into people from all walks of life. I mean you run into people who are 80, 70, 50, 40, male, female. Kids. They're all loving it.

INTERVIEW WITH
SABRINA LLOYD

BL: So, what role did you play in "The Wizard of Oz"?
SL: (Laughs.) The Scarecrow.

BL: Not Dorothy? (Laughs.) With a stage background before your movie and TV work, I'd imagine Sliders *would appeal to you for the variety of parts. Plus you get to do such different things because you meet your doubles in these other worlds.*
SL: Definitely. Stage gives you training that's wonderful in anything that you do. We do get to play many different parts on *Sliders*. That's one of the reasons that I was so attracted to the show and to Wade because the opportunities there for acting were just wonderful.

BL: I notice how, in "In Dino Veritas," you and the Quinn character hardly ever have to worry about the truth collars. You only get shocked when you deliberately lie, but poor old Rembrandt and Arturo are getting zapped all the time. Does this mean you guys are playing such goody-two-shoes characters that you'd be insufferable in real life?
SL: Well, I was attracted to Wade because she's a really good person. I don't think that it would be nauseous to be around her in reality, but I do think that she lives up to high moral standards. She is very honest and open. I think that's wonderful because we don't see that much in society.

*BL: Sliders is a very romantic show, and I mean that in terms of val-
ues. Do you think it was intended to be that way from the start?*

SL: Yes. Tracy is our creator and he brought these characters to life
that way and we all love him for it. I think he has an amazing
imagination that he brought to the show. We owe everything to
him.

*BL: Have you thought that kids might become interested in history
from watching the show?*

SL: Sure. I can see it interesting children in something that they
might not like otherwise. I've started reading more since being
on the show!

BL: How did you first find out about Sliders?

SL: It was pilot season, I was living in New York, and the script came
across my hands like, you know, a hundred other pilots that season, and it was the only script out of the entire year that I was,
like, "God, this is really interesting! This is different." I just immediately fell in love with the project. Luckily they fell in love
with me, too, because I got the job.

BL: Are you a science-fiction fan?

SL: I think I'm more so now that I've been doing a science-fiction
show. I started reading a lot of books about parallel universes
when I got the job, just to make myself aware of that kind of
story. I watch *Star Trek*, of course.

BL: You know Tormé was involved with Next Generation before this.

SL: Yes.

*BL: In material I was sent about him, there was a quote where he was
talking about how some of the characters on Trek were becoming*

bland. I don't think anyone will ever find the characters on Slid-
ers bland.

SL: Yeah. Not the way we argue all the time! But it helps that we can
disagree and still like each other. I think that the chemistry between the four characters really leaks over from the four of us in
person. We just genuinely like each other so much and we've
created a family, especially since we were shooting in Canada for
two years. We were all alone, all of us away from our families and
our friends, so we would have Thanksgiving dinner together and
we became each other's family. Like any family, you don't agree
about everything. But because we have this family kind of
thing, when they do create conflict on the show it's easy to play
off that. I really believe that these characters would do anything
for each other.

BL: Now here's a silly question. That's when you were shooting in
Canada. Now that you're shooting in Hollywood, will it all go to
hell?

SL: (Laughs.) No, I hope not. We've been here for a while now, and
it's still great. I mean, of course we all have our family and
friends so we don't spend as much time together off set as we
did in Canada, but we're still close.

BL: You and Jerry O'Connell are native New Yorkers?

SL: Yeah, I still live in New York.

BL: And does he, too?

SL: Yes. He graduated from New York University.

BL: Are there any special New York things between you?

SL: Well, since we're both New Yorkers, we have that camaraderie.
But we did not know each other before the show. We had different lifestyles.

BL: *Before we started taping, you mentioned you'd sent your family copies of my* Sliders *novel?*

SL: Yeah. We can put that in. I got them copies. I bought them in a bookstore in New York and sent them out.

BL: *You bought them?*

SL: I bought them. And sent them to my family.

BL: *I'm going to light a candle for you or put you in my will or something. I hardly know how to talk about this.*

SL: Excited as usual.

BL: *Yeah, I'm excited by that. I loved you as a hippy in "Summer of Love."*

SL: Oh, wow, that was back at the beginning.

BL: *I went to college during the final gasp of all that. So "Summer of Love" was a world I wanted to see. It's one of my favorite performances by you.*

SL: Well, it's funny, because "Summer of Love" was the first show that we shot the very first season. My first day on the set I'm dressed as a goddess and I have people worship me all day and I thought to myself, "You know, I think I'm gonna like this job a lot." (Laughs.)

I just felt caught up in this whirlwind because I've always loved the hippy era and I felt like I'd missed out on it. You know, it's like, oh, I would have loved to have been a part of it.

BL: *You're a hippy out of time.*

SL: A hippy out of time.

BL: *A flower child of the nineties.*

SL: Completely. So it was a lot of fun working on that. It was a great episode to just get us all in 'cuz we just loved it. We were having fun with it. We were hippies!

BL: *If I had to pick my favorite performance by you, I think it's "The Young and the Relentless."*
SL: Oh, yeah!

BL: *You are such a coldhearted bitch in that.*
SL: (Laughs.)

BL: *That is so much against what you're normally doing on* Sliders. *So tell me, did you have fun doing that?*
SL: I had a lot of fun. You know, you play a character for so long and people perceive you a certain way. So it was fun to go completely opposite and play this other Wade who was just a heartless bitch. As an actor it's challenging. It was a different Wade and yet it was still someone where you saw traces of the Wade we know.

BL: *The thing that really grabs me about this whole idea is how the same people can be so different in terms of the moral choices they make.*
SL: Oh, absolutely. I think about it all the time. What if I didn't make this choice? What if I made a different choice? Where will my life be ten years from now because of this choice that I am making? I don't know whether or not our choices are destined, whether we're going to make those choices whether we think we are or not.

BL: *And yet this show gives you a feeling of free will, doesn't it?*
SL: It does, but it's a tough one, 'cuz I don't know whether or not I'm gonna disregard destiny. I don't know. That's a question of the universe, isn't it?

BL: As a great thinker once said, we're predestined to have free will.
SL: There you go!

BL: This might be a good time to mention that I'm dedicating the book to Ken Steadman.
SL: Oh, wonderful.

BL: Can you tell me something about him for the book?
SL: I can tell you about the morning he died. I didn't know him that well. Our characters hadn't really worked together that much. But the night before the accident, we had seen a show, a preview of the premiere of *Sliders* because it was going to premiere the next night and we were all going to be working so we couldn't watch it. They had a little party for us and they showed the show. Then the next morning, we were in the makeup trailer and he just made me feel better than anybody about the show.

   We'd seen the premiere and I think I was a little bit frustrated by it, simply because it's hard for me to watch anything that I'm involved in. And he had such kind words for me and was such a supportive person. He said things like, "You guys have no idea how much you shine on camera. You should be really proud." I thanked him. He really made me smile. He was a wonderful man.

BL: I've never been clear on what qualifies as a stunt as opposed to the physical action the actors want to do themselves. There are plenty of stories about risks the big stars want to take on major motion pictures, and how the insurance companies are always worried.
SL: Yeah.

BL: Where do you come down on that? Do you have a daring streak?
SL: I did. I don't think that I'm as daring as I was because of what happened. I was very daring before. I was like, "I can do it. I can

do anything!" Then something like this shows you that accidents can happen at any moment and safety is more important than a short thrill.

BL: Let's talk about the future of Sliders. *Are you on for the duration?*
SL: I believe I'm on for the duration. I'm very happy doing the show. I'm very happy playing Wade. You know, so often when an actor works on a character, it's just natural for your character to seep over into your real life. Wade is such a great character. I've felt happier playing her in the last two years than, I think, any other role. Before Wade I'd played more tortured characters. I guess I was more tortured because of that. Now I'm having the time of my life. Yeah, I'll stay with it as long as it goes.

∞   ∞   ∞

I said the following in the September 1998 issue of *Femme Fatales*: "Sabrina Lloyd was wonderful, and I think it's a grave error that she's off the show. I'm not sure why she was replaced but I think it's a real tragedy."

INTERVIEW WITH
JOHN RHYS-DAVIES

BL: What do you think is the primary appeal of Sliders*?*

JRD: Asking "what if." That gave this show the potential to be the hottest show on television. It is limitless. Correction: The only limitations on it are the imaginations of the writers. That is a tribute to the remarkable nature of the concept, and, I think, an index of how far short the show has fallen from what it could be. Of the writers, I think Tormé is the only person who actually has an interest in science fiction. He's now sort of removed from the thing. The head writer we had last year was really more interested in writing propaganda for the ACLU than anything else. And there was a certain commissar-like approach to ideas and writing that I found completely repugnant, said so, and (laughs) endured the most miserable season for it.

BL: May I say that that's a bit ironic after the pilot episode about the commissars literally taking over America. Sliders *is one of the few shows in American television I've ever seen that dared to go outside the political-correctness cage. An example would be "The Lottery" episode, where right-to-life people were portrayed in a positive light. That's not typical television.*

JRD: That should be one of the techniques we regularly employ. We receive certain stereotypes through television, newspapers, our own prejudices, and one of the functions of a show like this should be to examine some of those stereotypes and startle us and surprise us. But there is a terrible tendency in any commercial medium—the idea that the real values of the universe

243

should be the values of the writer! Which is fine if you're writing *NYPD Blue* or something like that. But it's totally vacuous in trying to deal with the size of the universe and the potential of the universe. What good science-fiction can do is something quite different. Look at *The Demolished Man*. Or the great *A Canticle for Leibowitz*. I so want to make a film of *Canticle* one day. I think it's one of the finest pieces of science-fiction writing.

BL: *I was recently reading a book about the Irish monks who copied so much literature and saved a large part of Western civilization during the Dark Ages.*

JRD: Yes, indeed. But then as we Welshmen always like to observe to our Irish friends, St. Patrick was a Welshman!

BL: *Well, that's like the people who say all the great English actors are either Irish or Welsh or Scot, and then let's not forget Christopher Lee who's so very Italian.*

JRD: That's right. Dear Christopher, lovely man.

BL: *Of course, Peter Cushing, one of my favorite actors of all time, sure looked like an Englishman to me.*

JRD: Ah yes, and the great genius of the English is their language and the way that they have assimilated and best exemplified, I think, some of the Anglo-Saxon values. The notion of equality under the law.

BL: *Very different from equality of results. Poor America.*

JRD: I think that's one of the failures of English Common Law, and I think in a way I have more respect for the Napoleonic Code, the code of examining magistrates, rather than the form of interrogation that we have. The examining magistrate's function is to find out what really happened.

BL: *I know how to segue back into* Sliders. *So when the Arturo character is so upset at a French-occupied America in the "Invasion" episode, your heart wasn't really in that?*

JRD: (Laughs.) Well, no. I can forgive anything that is curious and genuine and springs out of ideas. What I find nauseating, repellent, and disgusting is this increasing and open consensus that the function of what a writer should do is go and watch movies and take notes from the movies and then try and work them into a script the next time. It's sort of officially blessed. I actually heard a producer the other day say, "I told him to go and read some science fiction and see if he can get some ideas there." I object to this sort of plagiarism—and that is what it is even if not in the strict legal sense. I recall my old professor of Scandinavian studies getting terribly into trouble in a review in the *Times Literary Supplement* when he actually said that of a fellow translator's work of Ibsen. The plagiarism problem is part of something larger. There is no sense of shame left in American screenwriting, and I would be embarrassed to hell if I wrote something and people said, "C'mon, *Twister* just came out and you've got twisters. I mean, is there any connection?" And why is it every script that you write has this one-on-one connection with a recent film? Or two recent films? The examples are endless.

BL: *It's the joke that in Hollywood everyone wants to be first to be second. I love Gore Vidal's comment that the old Hollywood screenwriters had the decency to steal from novels and stage plays, which were at least one level closer to real life.*

JRD: Right.

BL: *But today's screenwriters don't even steal from that source anymore; they only steal from other movies, so it's even more abstract, more artificial, and we lose the integrity of stealing from better sources.*

JRD: There's the episode where we were crossing a bridge and we looked down and it's completely invisible. You can see right through it. And I said, "Well, there's a film called *Indiana Jones and the Last Crusade* . . ."

BL: *Which you know something about.*

JRD: Which I have a little knowledge of. I suggested they should have Jerry say, "Wait a minute! I saw this in a movie! It's an optical illusion!" That becomes tribute.

BL: *Homage. God bless homage.*

JRD: That's right.

BL: *There's a more serious problem than not getting movie references when you're doing a show about alternate histories. What about an audience that doesn't know enough history to recognize when you change it? At least* Sliders *is entertainment that might interest people in finding out about real history. I'm sure there's a question in there* . . .

JRD: You would have that if you had writers who'd read any history or knew any history or could distinguish between fact and fancy. I'm not saying we haven't had any of that. But Nan Hagen did one where we're all road warriors in which she talked about Atlantis lying to the west of America and really being there! She became most indignant when I said that Atlantis is a myth. She dug out some piece of science fiction that she was offering as fact.

BL: *I always knew that Plato was a science-fiction writer. How can you play with history if you don't know what it is?*
JRD: Yes.

BL: *I've seen a number of episodes of* Sliders *with far higher standards than that. I'm sure about this after watching three seasons worth.*
JRD: Well, you can slay me for this, but I must tell you something. Consider a writer—we won't use names—who finds it really hard to come up with new ideas for the show and so the writer thinks we ought to go back and revisit some of the worlds that we missed opportunities on! I mean, this is just nonsense. We haven't started with this show.

BL: *All you need is an encyclopedia.*
JRD: My feeling is that we have not even begun to do the show properly. I got so fed up with our lack of ideas that I came up with four semi-original ones, pretty original ones, and suddenly they said, "Great, yes, with this one we could do a double episode." That was until they found out I wanted to write one and Sheenk!, the door comes straight down.

BL: *You've written, haven't you?*
JRD: I've written.

BL: *You have an academic background as well, don't you?*
JRD: My degree is in English.

BL: *Same here, and I've taught. I'll bet you have.*
JRD: Yes, I taught for a bit.

BL: Well, Professor, you must want to bring what you know to your work.

JRD: The response is so interesting. Because you realize that the writer-producer system exists not to make the best product but to perpetuate itself. There is so much money involved in being a writer-producer. If you can get in on that, the whole goal becomes protecting your position. If the show goes down, what you have done by networking is to connect with somebody else. You can cut into the deal, and that leads to the next deal. The prime function of the writer-producer is to keep other snouts out of the trough.

BL: It's the idea that everyone can write, just like everyone can do brain surgery.

JRD: I'm appalled by that. I'd be happy if the writer would write and let people who know about producing produce. I think the term writer-producer was invented by geeks who thought they couldn't get laid by just being known as a writer. "Producer" offers more promise—and power—to the unsuspecting target.

BL: I would like to see a John Rhys-Davies script produced.

JRD: Well, thanks. For better or worse, I have an idea of what the series could be about. We're talking science fiction now. Storytelling is a way of getting a society to dream. That's why even shoddy television shows are culturally important. The quality of the writer's imagination can influence the values of a whole society. Soon real people will be going into space to explore, to live, to die. One of the myths they will take with them is science fiction, the best examples of which raise questions about our conduct in the face of the unknown.

Alas, *Sliders* has lost its moral focus and strategy. It exists from episode to episode by living in the borrowed clothes of other people's stories, scenes, ideas.

∞ ∞ ∞

Since finishing my work on this book, I learned that John Rhys-Davies is off the show. It seems to me that this interview is an appropriate place for one of the most talented people involved with *Sliders* to have a last word. Otherwise, why have a book at all?

INTERVIEW WITH
JERRY O'CONNELL

BL: *Since you started your acting career at eleven, in* Stand By Me, *you must have wanted to be an actor when you were a kid, or did you just stumble into it ?*

JOC: I grew up in New York, and that's not only the actor's capital but it's a theater capital. So I was always involved in theater, as an after-school activity. I was in an acting class...

BL: *Did it grab you?*

JOC: Yes. Always in school and camp plays, it was something I really followed. They had this big cattle call for the film, *Stand By Me*. I wanted it and I happened to get it. It was really the right time and right place. That was such a success that it put me in a place in acting in film and television that gave me a break. I mean, it's something you don't normally come by.

BL: *It's interesting that your first mass-media exposure, this big Stephen King film, is a very writer-driven project where the writer really counts. Now you're the star of* Sliders, *which has been one of the smarter shows on television, starting with what Tracy Tormé did.*

JOC: He's the best! I've been in a good position, so far, where I have been able to choose what I want to do. I have the luxury of not really having a lot of bills come on me. I was living at home, I was going to school, and I could just pick and choose parts whenever I wanted. *Sliders* was a classic case of that. I was a junior in college and I knew I wanted to get back into acting. I knew that graduation was fast approaching. I was reading a lot of television pilots, and here was one that I really wanted to do. It was one of the only ones I auditioned for.

BL: *Were you already a science-fiction fan?*
JOC: Oh yeah!

BL: *What sort of science fiction do you like?*
JOC: I like early *Twilight Zone*. I like that a lot. And *Star Trek*.

BL: *A Rod Serling fan.*
JOC: I really like Rod Serling. Not only for his work with *The Twilight Zone*, but also for his television theater, like *Requiem for a Heavyweight*. I'm a big Rod Serling fan and a big sci-fi fan.

BL: *Zone would also bring you into science fiction through a focus on character. Serling always put the emotions in.*
JOC: I went to film school at NYU, where I studied to be a writer. So Serling has been one of my idols.

BL: *You and Sabrina are both New Yorkers, and you both started acting as kids. There's this on/off, endless variation of relationships between the characters. So I must ask about the chemistry between both of you as performers.*
JOC: The whole cast is the best. I'm sure everybody told you we get along more than I get along with most of my family members. We like being together.

BL: *I see it. I don't think acting could be that convincing.*
JOC: We really get along; we really have a good time. I think that comes across in the show. And hats off to Tracy Tormé for putting us together in the first place. He was a real coach to this team; he got everybody here.

BL: *So let's talk about him.*

JOC: This is Tracy Tormé's project, and he knows it better than anyone else in the world; and it's like I really can't imagine this
show without him. I don't think he'll leave the show. I think
he'll always be a major part of it.

BL: *What are some of the other creative people like?*

JOC: You know, we have a great bank of writers. Some of the scripts
are really cool. That's why it's such a fun show to do, because it
is so different than anything else on TV. It's different every
week. You will find yourself, when you're working in TV, doing
the same thing week after week, same story, on the same sets,
in the same situations. Whether it's a law office or a precinct or
an emergency room. But on *Sliders*, it's a whole different ball-
game, a different world every week.

BL: *Often feels more like a movie than television.*

JOC: It's like Rep. Theater with completely different scenarios . . .

BL: *I've noticed an almost father/son relationship between the Quinn
and Arturo characters. And Tracy put his dad into the "Greatfellas"
episode.*

JOC: There's a lot of that in *Sliders*. But also, the professor is my professor, you know? I am the student in the show. You can't really
get away from the whole father-and-son thing . . . and also because we're on this crazy adventure. It's just the four of us who
are really together. You really have to touch on the father/son
relationship. I love it because John is like my surrogate father
out here. I'm out in Los Angeles, I don't know anybody out here.
He even got me a car.

BL: *What kind?*

JOC: A truck. The Green Hornet.

BL: *I wanted to ask, since you play such a nice character, do you like it when you get to play a different version of yourself with a darker side?*

JOC: Yeah! The main appeal for me about doing the show was the fact that I was going to be able to come up with new characters. I wouldn't have to play the same character if this show goes ten years.

BL: *It's more like the old anthology shows where you could get into a lot of variety. Most series programs, as you just said, are doing the exact same thing every week. But this is an amazing combination: a series show that gives you the variety of an anthology.*

JOC: That's the main appeal to me.

BL: *Do you have a favorite episode?*

JOC: Yes. I really liked the episode where we went to a world where 90 percent of the population of men on the face of the Earth was wiped out from a disease. So the remaining 10 percent was used for breeding purposes. I like that ratio.

BL: *"Love Gods."*

JOC: Yes!

BL: *You're telling me you liked that better than "The Weaker Sex" episode, where men are second-class citizens?*

JOC: (Smiles.) That was a fun one. But I go with "Love Gods."

BL: *You've done stage work as well as film and TV . . .*

JOC: A lot of stage work; that's where I started.

BL: *Do you find that this show draws on theatrical elements in a way that a lot of episodic TV does not?*

JOC: It does because of the completely different scenarios. You're not playing one note the whole time. It's constantly changing. You have to change with it. It keeps you on you're toes, this show. You can't sit back and become a lazy TV actor.

BL: You may be playing the smartest guy in the world. Maybe the smartest guy in all these parallel Earths. The Arturo character is a brilliant man, but not a supergenius. The Quinn character is a super genius. And yet in a lot of science fiction of the past, the most brilliant character would be cold and emotionless, the Mr. Spock type. Here you are playing a very warm, nice guy on one hand and this incredible genius on the other hand. How do you combine those elements?

JOC: By focusing on his youth. I'm a twenty-two-year-old playing a twenty-five-year-old. I can relate to the youthful side of Quinn. However brilliant he is, I think generally all early-twenties males have a similar way of relating to the world and to other people.

BL: Do you think the character even knows what a genius he is? Or is he kind of oblivious?

JOC: Oh, I think he realizes how smart he is. I mean anyone who is getting a doctorate in physics, or is in grad school at Berkeley for physics, must realize that he's not an idiot. And then he makes the big discovery!

BL: I sometimes get the feeling that a really brilliant scientist type assumes that other people are smarter than they are.

JOC: At least Quinn has very intelligent companions. I think he knows he has a lot to learn, and that's what's so nice about his character is that he goes to these worlds without a superior attitude.

BL: He's not a know-it-all.

JOC: No, not at all. And you really can't be when you're going through different societies that you know nothing about.

BL: *That would teach humility, all right. What's your take on the Arturo character?*
JOC: I wouldn't say that the professor is egotistical. I'd say he's very proud of his title, Professor Maximillian Arturo ... as he should be. John is terrific at the role. I don't think they could have cast a better professor.

BL: *One of the top actors in the world. What's it like working with him?*
JOC: It's the best. I pinch myself every day. I've learned more from Rhys-Davies than, I can honestly say, any other actor I've ever worked with, or director or anyone else. He's taught me a lot.

BL: *I asked Sabrina what it's like playing such an honest character, with reference to the truth collars in the dinosaur episode. I'd like to ask you the same thing about Quinn.*
JOC: I don't know! I mean, I know that my character has sucker-punched a couple of people. That's a kind of dishonesty, I guess. But, I think he's put in these situations where he just doesn't have time to mess around. Maybe it's that he doesn't have time for the little lies.

BL: *He's very straightforward.*
JOC: Yeah. That makes for a good character in many ways.

BL: *One more thing about Quinn's mind. Wouldn't it be something to keep a count of five card decks in your head at the same time?*
JOC: That scene was a lot of fun, because whenever I do gamble I lose everything. But again, that's this show, you know. It's a blast.

BL: *How was it doing the scenes with Mel Tormé in "Greatfellas"?*

JOC: I couldn't believe I was working with Mel Tormé. I really hope he feels better. I know that he's been having some medical problems. But it was a real thrill for me. I think it was one of the best shows.

BL: *What was it like working with Ken Steadman? I'm dedicating the book to him.*

JOC: We worked on "Desert Storm." He was a terrific guy. One of these guys who always had a smile on his face. As an actor, he was willing to take any chances. He really had his craft down. I remember when I was working with him, I thought, "Wow, this guy has really got it." It was a shock to all of us when he died.

BL: *Is there any current project you want to mention?*

JOC: I have a movie coming out, *Jerry Maguire*. It is coming out in a couple of weeks, a Tom Cruise movie. I play a quarterback in that for the Broncos. That was a blast. That was every little American boy's dream come true.

BL: *And what about the cockroaches? Don't you want to mention them?*

JOC: Yeah, well, let's just say that after I did *Joe's Apartment*, working with all the roaches, I was very happy to come back to *Sliders* and see all my cleaner, better-mannered co-stars, Sabrina, John, and Cleavant! Working with the roaches was pretty gross.

BL: *Worse than the Spider-Wasps, huh?*

JOC: Yeah, exactly. You remember those?

BL: *You've been around some really good special effects, such as the allosaurus in "In Dino Veritas." What's it like when you're acting with stuff that isn't there?*

JOC: It's tough, but again, having gone to film school, I really love to see the tricks played out, and I love to see the final polished product of an episode. When you are acting to nothing and then you see the final product and there is, you know, a cockroach or a dinosaur, it's pretty amazing.

BL: *Vanessa, I promised you could ask a question.*

VANESSA KOMAN: *How did you like writing the* Sliders *comic book?*

JOC: It was a blast writing the comic book. I have been a big comic-book fan, and when I found out there would be a *Sliders* comic, I sent them a bunch of ideas and one of them hit.

VK: *It was cool.*

BL: *Do you have other writing plans? I want to get this in, too, because you and John are both writers as well as actors.*

JOC: Yes, I read a lot of screenplays. It is what I majored in at school. Right now I am just getting my chops down, pulling the way, having a good time, and, hopefully, maybe in the future, I'll write more.

INTERVIEW WITH
PETER SPELLOS

This interview was conducted before I started work on the episode guide. Instead of winding up in Cult Movies, *the film magazine for which I regularly write, this interview with a character actor who had a part on* Sliders *seems more appropriate for this book.*

Peter Spellos has always been lucky. In TV Land, he has at least one role more famous than his stint on Sliders. *He's the guy Teri Hatcher shoots on* Lois and Clark. *Fan translation: HE DID A SCENE WITH TERI HATCHER!*

For this book, Peter Spellos organized his answers about Sliders *into the following. So instead of the Q&A, here's something different.*

∞ ∞ ∞

Coming onto a show as a guest star can sometimes be an alienating experience. The cast and crew have been working together for a while and have already bonded into a close-knit unit. When you spend twelve to fourteen hours a day with the same group on location or in a studio, you feel like an outsider at a family function, invited to partake...but not really part of the core. This was not the case with *Sliders* in one important respect. Everyone went out of their way to be warm and gracious. As a character actor who often does villains, I have only one thing to say: A bad guy never had it so good.

By the third day of shooting, I felt like one of the gang. With only one week to shoot each episode, there was much to be done every day, but the atmosphere around the set remained relaxed. This made it a very creative and productive environment. It was also a pleasure to spend a week in Vancouver, a beautiful city to which I'd never been (and on my birthday, no less).

I enjoyed playing Jimmy Fountain on the "Eggheads" episode. Villains have always been more enjoyable for me than "do-gooders." I've played mob bosses and henchmen, and they are often stereotypical "dems" and "dose" kind of guys. But Jimmy was different. As different as the alternate Earth he lived on. When trying to convince Quinn to throw the big game, in order to offset a million-dollar gambling debt he owed, Jimmy suggested that, "Desperati desperandum faciunt." (Desperate men do desperate deeds.)

We shot the climax of the show that evening on the roof of the Canadian Broadcasting Company. The Sliders (except for John Rhys-Davies) and I had worked the past hour on the chase scene prior to the rooftop scene. Nothing like a nice pinstripe suit and a pair of Italian loafers to do aerobics in! After we completed shooting that scene and finished our dinner break, John arrived to shoot the finale. He's a very impressive man, both in stature and in presence. His mellifluous voice echoed through the halls of the CBC. We were waiting for the elevator when we were introduced for the first time. He greeted me with a firm handshake and a warm smile. We exchanged pleasantries and entered the elevator.

John and I are both men of joyous quantity. As we stood side by side (with not too many others around) during our ascent to the scenic skyline set, John turned to me and spoke in his rich, metered, baritone voice. "So you're playing the villain in this episode?"

I turned and responded, "Yes, I am, John." He put his arm around me and shook me in a fraternity brother–like fashion and bellowed, "Pound for pound, we're the best villains on the planet, aren't we?" I agreed whole heartedly, with every ounce (and pound) of conviction and joy I had.

AND NOW, THE PRODUCERS . . .

INTERVIEW WITH
TRACY TORMÉ

BL: *Tracy, I noticed in some of the material I was sent on you, that you had worked on* Star Trek: The Next Generation *for two years, and one of the problems was how the characters were so agreeable all the time that they were going bland. Was that one of the motivating factors for creating the interesting character dynamics of* Slid-ers?

TT: Yes, absolutely. I didn't want to do four dead-end characters who always agreed and always patted each other on the back and just went along seeing things the same way. We did that on *Next Generation* too much in the early going. Initially, we put Rembrandt in so he would be on the outs with the other three . . . because he was the innocent victim who was swept into this. I think in some of the early shows he is angst ridden about that; and then we started to establish the Wade vs. Arturo angle, where the professor is the skeptical scientific mind and Wade is the New Age '60s mystic sort of mind. That's where we put conflict into the show.

BL: *Does Quinn, as a supergenius, see both Wade's and Arturo's viewpoint?*

TT: That is true, but on the other hand, I think a lot of geniuses are kind of dense when it comes to other areas. In a lot of ways, Quinn has his own blind spots, especially towards Wade and in her attitudes about him and things like that. So, even though he is a supergenius in some ways, I believe that geniuses tend to be sort of childish in other ways. Quinn has his own personal foibles that he still has to work on.

BL: *You made him deliberately oblivious about certain routine human things?*

TT: In the sense that he is so into his experiment when the show opens that he is very blind to Wade's feelings towards him, that's for certain!

BL: *It seems that the Rembrandt character and the Wade character pick up on normal stuff a lot quicker than the Arturo or Quinn characters.*

TT: That's intentional in the sense that a lot of scientific people tend to see the world in blacks and whites, whereas Wade and Rembrandt would certainly be the most sort of everyman/everywoman part of the show. It's one of the ironies a lot of the time that even though they don't have the intellect of the other two, they have common sense. That can be just as important.

BL: *Speaking of seeing the world in black and white, one of the pleasures of* Sliders *is how right-wingers want to call it left-wing and left-wingers want to call it right-wing.*

TT: Yeah. That must mean we're doing something right.

BL: *You wrote both the pilot, with Communists taking over America, and "Summer of Love," with President Ollie North in a bad light.*

TT: I tend to find the far right and the far left equally ludicrous. The far right I just kind of feel sorry for. I feel like they are kind of ignorant about things. This is a generalization.

BL: *Give them a black helicopter for Christmas. (Both laugh.)*

TT: And the far left, which I am probably closer to at heart, I find to be the most dishonest now. I mean, the far left has to do lots of lying in order to support its positions. So, as far as the Communist thing went, it's ironic. On the one hand, Communism was a very bad thing. On the other hand, some people took fighting it to an extreme where they thought there were Communists influencing everything. We based the show partly on an old Jack Webb short film, I think it's called *Red Menace* or something like that...

BL: *I've seen it. It's called* Red Nightmare.

TT: We did a satirical, rather tongue-in-cheek portrayal of Jack Webb's nightmare of America, but still serious for all of that.

BL: *Judge Wapner's being in the pilot with* The People's Court *is a great gag, like something from your* Saturday Night Live *days. You wanted some comedy in this from the start?*

TT: That is really true and that has become lessened a lot, especially in this third season. This third season there's almost no humor at all in it. Weiss came from *The Naked Gun, The Blues Brothers,* and *Kentucky Fried Movie*—that's his background. He and I like putting in humor.

BL: *Sounds like a natural team.*

TT: My roots were in comedy, *SCTV* and *SNL,* and we both like sick, dark humor. So our idea was always to have that be a big part of the show. For instance, in "Fever," we did an infomercial for the plague world where—instead of being about sweaters or car wax—it was about home protection, sanitization units. But it was done exactly like a typical infomercial! That is what I wanted to do throughout the life of the show. The problem has been that doesn't really fit in the network and the studio's conception of what a science-fiction show should be. So it has always been something that I've done in spite of what they wanted.

BL: But it succeeded?
TT: Well, I thought so. I think it is what makes the show unique…

BL: So why do they object to something that succeeded?
TT: I think there is a desire on their part to be able to define the show more clearly as time goes on and put it into a little box. The fact that we had so much dark humor in it was one of the things I think made them uneasy. They always felt that satire makes it harder for people to get a grasp on the show, and I think that they have just slowly but surely wanted it to be more of a straightforward action/adventure show.

BL: Which makes it like every other show.
TT: In my opinion, that is what is happening in the third season.

BL: I'm sorry to hear that because what made Sliders *so important was its idiosyncratic personality.*
TT: That's what I wanted.

BL: Also, you worked in some educational elements. You probably interested more kids in history through Sliders *than any number of history textbooks or teachers. Are they going to take that away?*
TT: I'm glad you said that because I was never really interested in history when I was in school. It's taught in such a dull way. They emphasize dates and battles and other mundane things, and it's not interesting. After I left college, I started reading a lot more

and I found out that history was really interesting. A love of history that I developed in the last ten years is definitely a part of *Sliders*. In the episode you mentioned, "Summer of Love," there is a reference to the Battle of the Coral Sea, which I had read about recently and so I put that in. It is not that well known a battle, but it was a critical one in WWII. So I like to put those things in. I can't honestly tell you that the network doesn't want those things; that they say, "No history." That is one of the few mandates we have never gotten. But it is kind of tied into the concept to do alternate history.

BL: *Was "Luck of the Draw" the most controversial show you ever did? It created a context where most people would be on the side of right-to-life Catholic priests because of the lottery/euthanasia program. I think that episode took guts in today's America.*

TT: Not really much hot water from the viewing public at all. I mean, it's surprising how over the past couple of years we have had very few complaints, except the occasional, "You guys are left-wingers," or "You guys are right-wingers." I think if my hand is in the show, the three things that I like to attack—and it comes across, hopefully, in the humor—are the far right, the far left, and political correctness in general. I find political correctness to be just reprehensible and tremendously damaging to the country. Political correctness angers me because I find it so inherently dishonest. Like when Johnny Cochran got on Christopher Darden, saying, "How could you tell it was a black voice?" Sometimes you can tell if somebody is black by their voice, just as you can tell someone is Latin by their voice, or whatever, but to get in there and say there is no such thing, [that] it is racist to say that, there is an example of just a massive lie. In the Dark Ages, people lied about things and everyone was afraid to take on the Church and the government. This is the aspect of the Dark Ages that we have now.

BL: *There are still a lot of people who resist the Stalinization and Naz-ification of America. Of course, if you get people doing enough self-censorship, you no longer require direct censorship.*

TT: It's interesting what you said about the Soviets and the Nazis, because I also believe if you go far enough to the left and far enough to the right, you end up meeting. The more direct answer to your original question is that whenever we are doing satirical things, it is usually my hand in there, whether taking shots at the radical right or the radical feminists.

BL: *Something else I like about your show is how often it explores father/son relationships at a time when I think most mass media has lost interest in the subject—despite how much of world literature and myth and legend depend on it. I love how you worked your dad into the "Greatfellas" episode. And a father/son relationship is at the core of "The Guardian."*

TT: My dad got very sick, had a stroke right around the time that I had just written "The Guardian." So a lot of the themes in "The Guardian" scarily came into my life because there was a while when we thought we might lose him or he might never be the same. There was even a night my wife and I went out to watch a meteor shower in the desert with some friends, and he was at his lowest ebb at that point, and I had just written the scene which was added to the piece where Quinn and his younger self go out to look at the stars.

That was a scene that wasn't in the original script. We needed a bonding scene. So I wrote this scene where they are out there and they are talking about his father dying. It's about all the things a father wants to say to a son, or a son to his father, and now it's too late and you may never get to say them. All the themes in "The Guardian" were happening in my real life at the time.

BL: *How is he now?*

TT: He is getting better, thank you. But it was weird because he had never missed a day at work in sixty-six years. And now suddenly he is completely incapacitated at that time... and it was very strange because "The Guardian" was actually an old idea that goes back to the first season. It wasn't like suddenly anything that happened to him influenced that script, but it was just a weird synchronicity that themes of fatherhood and father/son were very much prevalent in that script at that time in my life. That is a very special show to me in a lot of ways.

BL: *I enjoyed your idea to make him a country and western singer.*

TT: We had talked about using him a lot, in different places—and Jacob Epstein, who was with us as executive producer second season, had thought of giving him the part of the Prime Oracle, which is the part that Isaac Hayes later played in one of our pieces.

BL: *"Obsession."*

TT: Yeah. I just felt like if we are going to use him and if he is going to do this, let's really have fun with it; let's have him play himself. So, once that was agreed, we were looking for what was the right vehicle for him. I thrust him into "Greatfellas"—I thought why don't I make him everything that he is not in this world? He is not religious, so I made him a Jesus freak; he never drinks, so I made him a drinker; he hates country music with a passion, so I wrote a country and western song for him. Finally, I had him say that he lives on a chicken ranch outside of Nashville. I remember when I was coming to him and telling him this, he was looking at me like... "I'm gonna be what?" I wrote this song for him called "Praying to Jesus," which he sings in it.

BL: *Impossible to forget.*

TT: And he kept trying...it was the funniest thing, he kept trying to change the song! I remember my wife and I were in Vancouver for the shooting and we would go into his trailer and he would go, "No, no, no, here's what I want to do with this song," and he'd take out his guitar and he'd play something. I'd go, "Will you please do my song the way it is?" Eventually he did. It's too bad that more of the song didn't make it on the air because the song was really funny and he did a very long, country scat segment where he combines sort of country music and jazz scat in the middle of it. He was great.

BL: *And then you blow him up!*

TT: The night we watched it, I had a big party at my house and everyone was horrified that I had blown my dad up in the second act, and when we went to that commercial everyone was like, "I can't believe you did that." I knew he was gonna come back, but I couldn't tell anyone that, so I was taking on the role of an ashamed son for two acts until at the end he steps out of the shadows and you see he is still alive.

BL: *They don't call it alternate history for nothin'.*

TT: Exactly right.

BL: *Jerry O'Connell was telling me he really felt there was good chemistry between him and Mel Tormé.*

TT: They really hit it off. My dad is a real pro, so when he went up there he knew his lines and he was very professional. He tries hard and he didn't go up there with an attitude like, "Jeez, I'm just doing this as a favor for my son." He really was into the part, and I think the other actors appreciated that.

BL: *One of your later stories was the Kromagg one. I thought the implications were terrifying in "Invasion" as to the military possibil-*

ities of sliding. What is the future of the show concerning the Kromaggs?

TT: Well, the problem with the whole ride on the show for me, and one of the reasons I'm leaving, is we never have really ever had anyone at the network that really understood what this show was and how to develop it further. My attitude was always: After the first season we've gotta do something new the second season. We've gotta create something new; we've gotta take the characters to new places!

I went in at the very beginning of the second season and pitched this whole idea about the Kromaggs. I said let's create a villain, a very specific sliding villain. They already have sliding technology, but they go from world to world to conquer. I gave them the whole thing and they just killed it on the spot. They later said, "We don't want to do Fascist World." I said, "What's Fascist World?" They said, "Oh, you know, that thing with the Kromaggs." So that was how they took it; they latched onto the idea that the Kromaggs were fascists, and somehow that got in the way of the whole idea.

BL: *Other worlds they've approved have just as many fascistic implications as the Kromaggs.*

TT: I was just angry that we couldn't do a show like this. I thought *Sliders* should be this boundless show that should be able to do almost anything, and all of a sudden we had these mandates: No politics, nothing too dark, nothing too this, nothing too that, not too science-fictiony! I mean it was all this stuff which made us... it was such a struggle to do shows that broke out of that mold. So I went to the head of the network. I had a lunch with him and basically talked about several things I was kind of dissatisfied with, but one of them was, "Why can't I do this show?" And he said, "Well, I wasn't even aware of this show. If this means that much to you, do it." So, basically, he overruled his underlings and I did the show. In fact, I was writing "Post-Traumatic Slide Syndrome" at the time. That was my show.

BL: *That is the most paranoid, don't you think, of all the episodes? Because fans are still arguing which Arturo went with them, and that's P-A-R-A-N-O-I-A.*

TT: Yeah, that's fun.

BL: *I'm assuming it's the good Arturo.*

TT: I'm never gonna tell on that one. (Both laugh.) I wrote "Invasion" very quickly, and it was kind of a test for us. Could we really do a big sci-fi show for our budget and make it pay? The original version of "Invasion" had a lot more things that we had to cut out.

BL: *It still feels like a movie.*

TT: Good. The point is that you have to pick your fights; otherwise, you get this reputation of being difficult if you argue with them all the time about everything. So I have had to be careful about that because there was a time early in the second season where I really was doing a lot of arguing with them about a lot of things.

BL: *Was Conrad Bennish part of that?*

TT: Yes, Jason Gaffney and I became good friends, and our wives travel together. He's a funny and very good actor. The network started taking him out of all the scripts we had him in. They just didn't like him. They kept comparing him to a character on VR5 who had long hair. So they said, "Here's another long-haired character." I tried to explain. I don't think the character on VR5 can build atom bombs, then go to his room and listen to Grateful Dead music. They cut him out of everything. He was in three or four of the scripts and they just said, "No, we don't want Bennish in this."

So I put him in "Invasion," despite the network. We didn't call him Bennish! We went to him and said, "We're gonna put you in a cage. They've taken your eyes out. It's gonna be spooky. It's gonna be weird. The audience isn't really going to get a look at you until the last shot, and they'll see you have no eyes." We didn't know how many people would recognize him. Anyway, that's how we got around the network.

BL: *It's amazing some of the things you have to fight.*
TT: Yes, it is.

BL: *Well, I love the way you kept working in Pavel Kurlienko, the recurring taxi driver. No matter how different the parallel Earths, good old Pavel always has the same job.*
TT: (Laughs.)

BL: *How difficult was it to put together the quartet with the kind of chemistry they have?*
TT: We were very lucky. They are very professional and their egos are not huge. They want the show to be good. What probably comes across on the show is how easy they are to work with. Of course, I'd had this experience before on *Star Trek: The Next Generation* where the cast had chemistry together.

BL: *I've found that a lot of people who generally don't like science fiction find* Sliders *appealing. You've tapped into something on the order of* The Day the Earth Stood Still *and the original* Invasion of the Body Snatchers. *The characters connect with the audience. The premise of the show allows you to explore every genre—a continuing character series with the advantages of an anthology show.*

TT: A true observation. *Sliders* is an anthology show with recurring characters.

BL: *When you have something like this, who would want to fix it?*

TT: Everyone. The double-edged sword of *Sliders* is that it's all things to all people. The network has never been clear on what the show is. They worry about what it's not supposed to be. I always knew it was science fiction. I've always liked SF. I find a lot of stuff on television so restrictive. Who wants to see another cop show, another detective show? They've been done to death—so for me, the reason I like to do science fiction is similar to the types of comedy I did before. I wouldn't want to do sit-com for the same reason I resist formula drama shows. There's nothing more restrictive than a sit-com half hour.

The type of comedy I did on *SCTV* and *Saturday Night Live* was wild. You could go after anything at any time. Science fiction offers the same freedom, and that's what we've tried to do in *Sliders*. The fact that our show takes place on other Earths is the only reason we can get away with some of the stuff we do. Whenever there's something touchy going on, like with the feminist show about the world dominated by women, it's only by stressing we're on another Earth that we could have the freedom to do the satire we did.

BL: *A number of my friends collect more British SF series than they do American because they find more wit and extrapolation in the former. They consider* Sliders *an exception worth collecting.*

TT: I really appreciate that. *The Prisoner* is one of my all-time favorite shows.

BL: *Same here. It's certainly the most libertarian TV series ever made.*

TT: Recently Patrick McGoohan heard I did a show called "The Schizoid Man" on *Trek*. I named the show after my favorite *Pris-*

oner episode. So he called this office—he knows my assistant a
little bit—and I got on the phone with him thinking I'd talk to
him for thirty seconds (I was actually pretty nervous to talk to
him), and we talked for half an hour. We discussed *The Prisoner*,
and I told him about the influence it had on me. It creeps into
a lot of my work, like "Invasion" we were just talking about.
There's a lot of *The Prisoner* in that episode when the characters
are being interrogated and tricked. The aliens want information
from them they don't want to give.

BL: *The Prisoner is a good influence on the writing of dialogue. Like
the time Number 6 is accused of not having any values and he responds, "Different values." Or when someone accuses Number 6 of
advocating anarchy and he answers, "Hear, hear."*

TT: I think McGoohan at heart must be a libertarian. A lot of that
comes through in the show. I know you're a libertarian and I
have libertarian tendencies myself, especially on social issues.
Technically, I'm an independent—an ex-Democrat. The official
Libertarian position is a little too isolationist for me. And I don't
believe in some of the Open Borders stuff because I think that's
kind of naive myself.

But, having said that, I really believe in the basic libertarian
idea that you should be allowed to do what you choose so long
as it doesn't hurt anybody else. I don't believe the government
has the right to interfere with you the way it does today. I also
agree with the libertarians that the war on drugs is the biggest
sham in the world. They keep spending more and more money
on it; and putting people who are nonviolent criminals in the
jails while letting serious offenders out early. It's a ridiculous
system, skewed by the religious right, among others ...

BL: *It's Prohibition, Part 2, and does just as well as the original
model.*

TT: Exactly. It's a scam. I voted for Harry Browne (the presidential candidate of the Libertarian Party). I did it mostly as a protest but I liked him a lot. Domestically, I'm with the Libertarians on about 90 percent of this stuff.

BL: *This relates back to* Sliders *because in normal politics you're told you have only two choices when neither may reflect what you actually believe.* Sliders *exercises the imagination by showing different political and social possibilities.*

TT: The sad thing is just how entrenched are the Powers That Be. The Democrats and the Republicans and major institutions have a lock on it. When someone like Harry Browne talks on television or the radio, I believe the great majority of the audience thinks he is making total sense. Yet many of these same people won't vote for him. They end up voting for someone they like a lot less than Browne.

BL: *They're afraid a Libertarian victory would slide us into a world for which they're not prepared—real freedom and real responsibility.*

TT: Fear is a large part of it. The whole system is based on people's not wanting to rock the boat. It's disappointing. I always hear the same parties talk about the progress they're making. I hope that's true, but it's hard to see on election night. They are so totally ignored by the media. The way it's so hard to get into the debates...there is something almost un-American about that. If we ever had the Sliders find a libertarian world, it would be the closest they'd come to Utopia as far as I'm concerned.

In the pilot, Quinn's double mentions a world like that, and how he hopes he can find it again. Maybe that's a libertarian world. By the way, to add to what I said before, if the whole world accepted these principles, we wouldn't need to have an aggressive military and then I wouldn't have my problems about libertarian foreign policy.

BL: *Moving from the subject of dinosaur-like political parties to just plain dinosaurs, I must ask about "In Dino, Veritas," my favorite choice of title. Those special effects were tremendous.*

TT: Yeah, we're proud of the look of the allosaur.

BL: *That's the episode also including the truth collars.*

TT: The concept of that goes back to my *Star Trek* days, when we were going to bring in a new character to replace the doctor. I had created a character who comes from an alien planet where truth is always told. Regardless of circumstances, they are 100 percent truthful at all times. I remembered telling Rodenberry: think how cool this would be if we could play off this like you played off Spock. How would truth 100 percent of the time affect people? And this guy is a doctor on top of it. If there's something wrong with you, he's not going to sugarcoat it. He's going to tell you exactly what it is. For various reasons, it didn't happen, but I loved the idea. The collars allow for the same kind of interplay.

BL: *I was fascinated by the truth collars.*

TT: Steve Brown came up with the idea of the truth collar. I lobbied for a much bigger scene in the opening. In the original version, there was a much longer period with the truth collars. In the complete version, Wade gets out of the car with Geraldo Rivera. She's been dating him on this world and told him about sliding. Since no one lies without being found out, he assumes her story is true and has decided to slide with them. He wants to videotape the next world and use it on his show. We were going to get Geraldo to play himself—and play it very egotistical. Very unlike real life, right? (Laughs.) He lands in the next world and they all ask him what he did—and he explains his plans to videotape it . . . and that's when they tell him there's no way to send him back. He says, "You never told me." He never asked. So he's stuck with them. Guess who gets eaten by a dinosaur?

BL: *Do you think it would be interesting to put truth collars on network executives?*

TT: If you did that, you'd have to empty out the jails. The scary thing is that they believe what they believe. It's not like lying in that sense. The problem is their attitudes. You have to luck out and get the right one. There is an executive at Fox who is very sympathetic to the show and understands what we were trying to do, but he's never been in the position of calling the shots. Television is a great double-edged sword. On the one hand, it's miserable—so under-utilized. One show has a certain following and they try to make six more copies of it. That's the bad side.

The good side is all about the opportunities. If you can do something that is at all smart, and get it on the network, everyone will say it's unbelievably smart and that there's nothing else like it. I want to keep doing smart shows. I'm talking with Lavar Burton about doing *The Seekers* as a cerebral show. Now I don't want to ever be in the position of saying something is too cerebral! I want my shows to get people to think but I also know the realities. You try to save what you can through the winnowing-down process.

BL: *Does your work in satirical comedy help when your trying to work clever bits into a dramatic program?*

TT: When you were doing the novel, we talked about the Judge Wapner scene because that's a funny scene in the show. He was in the pilot episode because Bob Weiss and I are big *People's Court* fans. We used to stop our meetings just to watch it. It's one of the funniest shows on television. The human nature that comes out in that show is tremendous. I put that in the script as an inside joke between Bob and me.

BL: *There really needed to be a Marxist-Leninist version of* The People's Court.

TT: Wapner agreed, but then the network came in and said we couldn't do it; it's too silly, too over the top—it changes the tone of the show—no one will like it. That's one of those things we had to argue.

BL: *You must have had a dèja-vu feeling when we talked over the phone about how I'd been asked to leave out the Wapner gag in the novel. Thanks to your intervention, it went back in.*

TT: I don't know who it is they're worried about. It often comes down to their not wanting the audience to think too much. That was one of the big rags on the second season from the network. It was too cerebral. When I hear that, I feel like quitting and getting another job. We should be proud there's stuff on there that make people think a little bit.

BL: *When they say "cerebral," they're not complaining about lectures, are they? The material they don't like has dramatic and emotional value.*

TT: I have anecdotes proving that for almost every episode. One example is "Greatfellas," the one with my dad where we did the joke about his being a country and western star. They said, "Look, people aren't going to get that. Can't he just be sitting at the piano..." They wanted him to be like he is here and not take advantage of the concept.

They're afraid *Sliders* is going to confuse people. Sliding is about going to other worlds. Fox is much more hands-on than any other network, and they say they can't afford any of their shows to go south with the ratings; they admit all this and they're open about it.

BL: *Why do they think everyone has to get everything?*
TT: They don't appreciate some of their greatest successes. Part of the success of *The Simpsons* is that it works on different levels. You can watch it with a little kid and a lot of stuff will go over the kid's head but he doesn't enjoy it any less. I always wanted *Sliders* to be that way.

Some of our writers said that when they took the pilot out of the house their kids started crying and wanted the tape back. So I said, "Wow!" We heard that on several occasions. I know the show is colorful and fast moving. Children will like it. But if we're doing stuff children don't pick up on, where's the harm? The show should not restrict itself.

Brad Linaweaver (left) with Tracy Tormé.

INTERVIEW WITH
ROBERT K. WEISS

BL: It's a pleasure to be talking with the man who helped develop The
Vanessa Angel Show, *otherwise known as* Weird Science.

RW: Thank you very much. She is worth watching every week.

*BL: The longest interview I've done for the book is with Tracy Tormé,
but I'm sure there's material you'll want to add.*

RW: Sure. It was all my idea! (Both laugh.)

BL: What's it like to go from producing the Naked Gun *films to working on a science-fiction series? Is there a common denominator?*

RW: It's always difficult when you're doing a weekly television series. I can't think of anything that's harder. When you're doing
a movie, you have more time. Theoretically, you don't start
shooting until the material is fully developed. In television, the
clock is much more severe. There are air dates, and you have to
be ready in time. Episodic TV is a voracious monster that has to
be constantly fed. The trick is to crank it out and still have it be
a quality effort.

How you mix comedy and reality is a question of how you anchor the comedy. The parody of *The Naked Gun* is so successful
because it sets up, in a very earnest way, expectations based on
archetypes with which the audience is familiar. We then reverse
the expectation in a surprising and hopefully funny way.

BL: Doesn't Sliders *reverse expectations also?*

RW: In the sense that we try to avoid being predictable. Reversing expectations is part of that. We try to keep it fresh.

BL: *Tracy says that it's a series show with the variety of an anthology. How did you both come to work on this?*

RW: I had for some time been thinking of doing this type of show with variety and longevity built into it. I'd been looking for a vehicle uniquely suited to the episodic demands of television. Started thinking about the idea as *Time Tunnel* sideways. Tracy and I had met on a UFO project and I told him about one of my favorite stories, "By His Bootstraps." Wasn't that by Anson Mac-Donald?

BL: *That was a pseudonym for Robert A. Heinlein. He was writing so much for* Astounding *that the editor, John Campbell, suggested that he use a pseudonym for some of his stories.*

RW: How wonderful. What a writer. "By His Bootstraps" was a story where the main characters are all the same guy meeting himself as he travels in time. That stuck with me. Combined with my interest in the "new" physics and alternate realities, the idea of parallel Earths became very appealing to me. Serendipitously, as Tracy and I were discussing the show, *Discover* magazine had a cover depicting parallel Earths. In fact, there are echoes of that cover in the original title sequence.

Of course, there were changes from the first conception. Originally it took place in a boarding house in Seattle with a lot of characters. As we worked on it, we came up with the idea of three characters whose lives were already connected, and a new character who was pulled into the story by happenstance.

BL: *Were you trying for educational value, slipping in history lessons?*

RW: That's a free lunch that comes with the show. I'm fascinated by history, and *Sliders* is a unique franchise to present alternate versions. Do you remember *Mad* magazine's "Scenes We'd Like to See" department?

BL: *Yeah. Alfred E. Neuman lives.*

RW: My mentor. The first five panels of this department would set up a genre, a western or whatever. In the last panel, there would be a spin, an unexpected outcome. The humor would come from the spin. *Sliders* is the same thing. What if communism beat capitalism? What if? This is how we pitched the series. People who like science fiction got the idea of parallel universes right away. But for people without a sci-fi orientation, the concepts needed a lot of explaining.

Rather than become bogged down in exposition, I sold the sizzle—the scenes we'd like to see. That's how we hooked the network.

BL: *Can't you get away with any amount of scientific explanation if there's a spectacular special effect on the screen?*

RW: The technical aspect can be interesting so long as we remember it's not the meat of the show. You don't want to have dry talking heads. It often comes down to the balance . . . the combination of humor and science. If you can work in a good, fresh visual effect, so much the better.

BL: *This seems a good spot to give a plug to the special effects. The vortex is splendid. What's the story on it?*

RW: In terms of the look of the wormhole and the slide, that was done by a very talented guy named John Allison who was working at Stargate Films. We worked together on its creation. The appearance of the wormhole was based on its function, origin, and production economics. Tracy and I would see elements every step of the way. Nothing went out the door unless Tracy and I were both happy with it. That's the heart of a good collaboration and the only way to do a good show.

BL: *That leads into a question about the stars and how well they seem to work together.*

RW: We knew the key to the cast would be the actor who played Quinn. We wanted someone who could be a leading man with youth and energy and also be believable as a really smart guy. We were incredibly lucky to find Jerry.

The same thing happened with Rembrandt. This was an unusual character. We wanted him to be flamboyant without becoming a cartoon. Cleavant came in to audition and knocked our socks off. He did the scenes but he also sang "The Star-Spangled Banner" in character. He had the chops in his own career for the singing and the character of Rembrandt—as well as unbelievable charm and personality.

With the part of Wade, we didn't want to go the conventional route. A lot of women you see on TV fit a particular mold that we felt just isn't real enough. We wanted someone who was earnest and real. We loved Sabrina's energy and enthusiasm. That eagerness was in contrast to the professor, who at first is very cautious and frankly kind of scared. It was great to have this diminutive gal who is eager to explore new worlds vs. the stuffy, super-smart professor who is overcautious.

BL: *Are Wade and Quinn not only supposed to be young in years but in outlook as well?*

RW: Absolutely! It keeps the show fresh. We could develop so many things between them and their other selves on other worlds, including romance if need be. For the professor, we wanted someone who would lend instant credibility to the role so that the moment you saw him, you knew who this guy was. John certainly fit the bill.

BL: *Do you have a favorite season?*

RW: The first. It's when most of the invention happened. I think it's the season where we took the biggest chances and tried to push through the boundaries. We experimented, tried different mixes of humor, action, and story. We showed a number of different worlds in a single episode, often ending on an open note in another place... instead of the last shot only showing them disappear into the vortex. I'd like to see the show return to more of its roots.

BL: *Maybe all the episodes should be judged against the pilot.*

RW: It may well be the best barometer. We had to fight for the pilot story. The position of the networks was that people wouldn't be interested in what we called Red World—a place where Communism had taken over. We knew in our gut that people would be interested. The network was stubborn. We were able to insist and got our way. To their credit, they recognized that it did ultimately work.

BL: *Seems that anything not the same as every other show is automatically controversial.*

RW: Controversy tickles us the most. It means people are thinking about the show and reacting to it, instead of the blah reaction that so much television gets and deserves.

BL: *Was there a policy from the beginning about how to deal with some of the more adult subject matter that Sliders slides up against?*

RW: When you're an 8 o'clock show, there are some general characteristics a show needs to have. One of the things we had to take into account was that if Fox decided to move it, it might end up as early as 7 o'clock on a Sunday evening. This meant there were themes and approaches to material that had to be softened. We suffered from that.

BL: *Any last thoughts about the primary strength of this show?*

RW: I think it's great that people can watch the same show and have completely different views about the meaning of the story. When we started this project, there was very little science fiction on TV except for space opera—you know, variations on *Star Trek*. Then as we started, *X-Files* came on. But we couldn't use that as a precedent because the network always referred to that show as a special case. There is a lot more science fiction on television now. In addition, more people are familiar with the science side of sci-fi. In fact, physicists can't make quantum physics work unless there are multiple universes.

BL: *Will mankind ever figure out how to slide?*

RW: I hope so. Count me down and let's slide!

ABOUT THE AUTHOR

Brad Linaweaver is the author of *Sliders: The Novel*. He is co-author, with Dafydd ab Hugh, of four bestselling *Doom* novels, based on the phenomenal video game from id Software. He is the author of the award-winning novel *Moon of Ice*, and has sold over sixty short stories to anthologies and magazines. His nonfiction has appeared in a wide variety of publications, including *National Review*, *The Atlanta Journal-Constitution*,  *Chronicles*, *Cult Movies*, *Filmfax*, *Femme Fatales*, *Forrest J. Ackerman's Spacemen*, *Prometheus*, *New Libertarian*, and *Reason*. He shares original story credit on Fred Olen Ray's production of *Jack-O* (Triboro Entertainment) and co-edited with Ed Kramer a major science fiction anthology for Tor Books, *Free Space*.